The Back Forty
Farm Life in the Ottawa Valley

By Steve Evans

With B. Sibbald

GSPH

Published by

GSPH GENERAL STORE
PUBLISHING HOUSE INC.

1 Main Street, Burnstown, Ontario, Canada K0J 1G0
Telephone (613)432-7697   Fax (613)432-7184

ISBN 0-919431-37-2

Printed and bound in Canada.

Designed by Marlene McRoberts, Hugh Malcolm and Bill Slavin

General Store Publishing House Inc. gratefully acknowledges the assistance of the Ontario Arts Council.

Canadian Cataloguing in Publication Data

Evans, Steve, 1955-

  The back forty : farm life in the Ottawa Valley

ISBN 0-919431-37-2

  1. Farm life—Ottawa River Valley (Quebec and Ont.) 2. Farmers—Ottawa River Valley (Quebec and Ont.)—Biography 3. Agriculture—Ottawa River Valley (Quebec and Ont.)—Societies, etc. 4. Farmers—Ottawa River Valley (Quebec and Ont.)—Biography—Pictorial works. 5. Ottawa River Valley (Quebec and Ont.)—Biography. 6. Ottawa River Valley (Quebec and Ont.)—Biography—Pictorial works. I. Sibbald, Barbara, 1958- II. Title.

FC2775.E85 1990   971.3'8'00992   C90-090439-9
F1054.09E85 1990

First Printing November 1990

This book is dedicated to Bill Evans
June 26, 1919 — April 3, 1983

If you haven't got roots
You ain't got nothin'

And to Kelly

Acknowledgments

Many thanks to:

Tim Gordon, my publisher,

Barbara Sibbald, editor and author of the personality profiles in this book,

Marlene McRoberts, designer and production artist,

And the rest of the staff at GSPH Inc.

Special Thanks to:

Ilford Photo (Canada) Limited.

Jim Gauvreau.

And all the farmers who had to stop their work to answer my questions.

The front cover photograph is of Dale Gillan, Arnprior

The back cover photograph is of Bob Ferguson, Castleford

Introduction

This book is about a way of life: how some farmed years ago and how they farm today; why they farm and why their children will take over the farm. They are not well-known people but they are the roots of our community. Farmers do what they have to do and are proud of it. This book is about the farmer.

Steve Evans

Table of Contents

Chapter One

From Sunrise to Sunset

"It depends on the season."

It's the calm before sunrise in the Ottawa Valley when lights suddenly shine from the bedrooms of the Streight family's three homes. Robert Streight switches off his radio alarm at five o'clock. "I listen to the news and sports and I get up. We can milk fifty cows in an hour."

For Robert, his father Ransford and uncle Ralph, it's the start of another day on their Oxford Mills dairy farm. Robert's younger brother, eighteen-year-old David, also helps out when he's home from Kemptville Agricultural College.

It's an unrelenting business. Day after day, morning and evening, the Streights must be there to milk, feed and tend to their cows. On a normal day, if all goes well and if there isn't any crop work to do, the Streights work twelve hours, from five in the morning till six-thirty at night, with an hour off for dinner. Other days, during haying for instance, eighteen-hour days, from pre-dawn to sunset, aren't uncommon.

The family milks fifty-five Holsteins and raises another hundred and twenty-five calves, yearling heifers and two-year-old heifers, in their cow-calf operation. They also keep about twenty-five laying hens year-round and, in the summer, they raise thirteen turkeys and seventy meat-type birds for their deep-freezer. Robert's mother Marion looks after the poultry and the house, and also does a lot of running around the countryside, picking up machine parts and odds and ends, when the men are busy. Everyone helps out in the garden. For the Streights, farming is a family business.

"Eggs, milk, meat, vegetables — you name it, we grow our own," says thirty-three-year-old Robert, who is obviously pleased with the family's self-sufficiency.

It's still dark when Robert, Ransford, Ralph and David meet at the barn and begin setting up for milking. There isn't much need for conversation, everyone knows the routine. The barn is equipped with a pipeline milker which runs the length of the two rows of cows. Robert and Ransford grab two milkers a piece. They clean each cow's udder and attach the milker. "Fresh cows might give more milk and some milk faster," comments Robert. Each cow gives about six thousand litres of milk a year.

Half-way down his row, Robert pauses. "You've got to be efficient if you're in the dairy industry because we have what we call a cost-of-production milk formula. The Ontario Milk Marketing Board takes the information from dairy farmers across Ontario including feed costs for that particular farm, and hydro, labour costs, machinery and all like that. Then they take the information from the top seventy per cent most efficient farmers and average it in and determine what we're going to be paid for milk, whether we should have an increase or a decrease."

"You've got to manage, you've got to be efficient to stay in the business."

Being efficient in the dairy business means continually upgrading the herd to get more, high-quality milk from each cow. "The better heifers we supposedly keep for replacements for ourselves and the other ones are sold as springers," says Robert. "We now have eighty-per-cent pure-breds. Every year you're getting better cows, better bred. The dairy industry is big business."

At eight o'clock, when most people are just heading out to their jobs, the Streight family has already put in three hours of work and is ready to sit down to a breakfast of eggs, toast, coffee and milk. It's their last break until noon.

11

Marion, Ransford, Ralph and Robert Streight.

By 8:20, the men are back in the milking barn, cleaning up and looking forward to the arrival of Percy McFarlane who picks up their milk every second day. He arrives promptly at nine o'clock and the men pause a moment to consider the weather and the cows as Percy pumps the milk into his truck.

"As far as quality standards in milk goes, Ontario and Canada are second to no one in the world and they're continually getting better," says Robert. "If you don't have a good quality product, you get penalized and you don't get paid a top price. The consumers are after the top quality and that's the thing you have to maintain in the industry too."

With their milk quota and ensured monthly income, the Streights are more fortunate than many other farmers, who often can't make it on their farm income alone. At least two-thirds of Canadian farmers have to work off the farm. For these farmers, not only is there the usual uncertainty about the weather, there's the added pressure of another job and the constant worry about how much their crops or livestock will bring. Whether they'll break even, make a profit or lose money, depends on the market and that's out of their control.

The uncertainty is taking its toll. In 1976 there were 7,844 farmers on the Ontario side of the Ottawa Valley; by 1986, there were 6,312. Nineteen per cent of the farms in 1976 have been bought out by other farmers, sold for development or closed down. Some of these once-fertile acres are now growing over with junipers and poplar and will eventually revert to the same type of forests which the first settlers painstakingly cleared.

The success of the Streight Farm depends on all family members contributing.

At 5 a.m., the milking begins.

Among these were Robert Streight's great-grandparents who immigrated to the area from Ireland in the early 1850s. Over the next eighty years or so, the family built up a thriving farm in Augusta Township. Then, in 1937, Robert's grandparents, John and Florence, and their six sons, including Ransford and Ralph, moved five kilometres north-west to the family's present farm near Bishops Mills.

The Streights resisted pressure from the provincial government to sell the original one-hundred-and-twenty-acre homestead. Surrounding that farm is fifty-year-old Limerick Forest, a provincially protected area. Robert says their original land is part of the family's farming tradition. "That first summer, when the Streights came from Ireland, they pitched a tent. Then they lived in a shanty for a few years and then a larger log house was built. The house was torn down but the barn is still there and the land is good. Our children will be the fifth generation of farmers there," says Robert proudly.

Like the Streight family, many Ottawa Valley farm family's roots are in their land: a legacy from their fathers, grandfathers or great-grandfathers. Settlement began when the Napoleonic Wars ended in Europe in 1815 and unemployed soldiers and sailors were encouraged to immigrate to Canada. Later, the construction of the Rideau Canal, from 1826 to 1832, and the growth of the lumber industry brought prosperity and more people to the Valley.

"I've heard people say that as far as this land goes, before our ancestors took it over, it didn't grow hardly anything," says Robert. "Now we have no problem pulling off a first cut of a hundred bales per acre and going back for a second or third cut of hay and cutting off forty, fifty bales in the second, sometimes thirty or thirty-five. It depends on the season. It depends on the fertilizer you put on and it depends on the field."

In addition to the four hundred and five acres they own, the Streights rent another sixty. Robert says about three-quarters of it is tillable.

"When the haying season's on we could stand another hand because you like to get the hay off as quickly as possible. As July draws near, the protein content of the hay drops off, and when the protein content drops off it means that next winter the cows aren't going to give as much milk or you'll have to buy protein supplement from the feed store which costs you more," says Robert.

The men finish cleaning and putting away the milking equipment so it's ready for the evening

After milking, the barn is swept. Even the small jobs are shared by everyone.

milking and then move on to the calf barn to clean up there.

"As far as corn goes, last year on seventy-five acres we came off at about one hundred and thirty bushels of dry corn per acre. I think the average for Grenville County might be one hundred now.

"We take a soil sample at least every second year and we know what fertilizer is required. You've got to feed it to get it back.

"I have to keep records on the fields - how much fertilizer, how much corn - because if I don't, in a year's time, I won't remember. You put the right fertilizer on, you put the crop in when you should

get it in and you use the right spray to get rid of all the weeds and grass or your yield's going to suffer. And barring any major storms or anything abnormal that Mother Nature might deal us, we should get a pretty good crop."

There's no crop work to be done on this overcast, mid-July day, but that doesn't mean that the Streights can take it easy. "There's always something to do," Robert says matter-of-factly.

After cleaning the calf barn, they decide to put in a few hours repairing fences. They work for an hour or so with a chain-saw, putting points on cedar posts. The working day is half over and they head to the house for dinner.

After morning chores, the men appreciate the hardy breakfast Marion has prepared.

At 8 a.m., the men come in from the barn for breakfast.

At 8:20, it's back out to the barn and back to work.

Robert watches as Ransford loads manure to be spread on the fields later in the day.

Every other day, Percy McFarlane arrives at 9 a.m. to transport the milk to the dairy.

Percy takes a milk sample before pumping it into his truck.

The men make time during the busy day for a little conversation.

At 9:30, Ransford begins to clean the calf barn.

David carries fresh straw for bedding.

Working together makes the chores easier.

Ralph prepares to take a load of manure to the fields.

At 10:30, they begin to point cedar logs for fence posts.

Marion takes her butter tarts out of the pans.

At 11:30, Robert and Ransford open the mail.

Marion prepares the noon meal.

The dinner table is set.

At one o'clock, it's back out to the barn.

The posts are taken to the field where the men begin work on a new fence.

Ralph and Ransford line the posts up.

Most of the afternoon is spent working on the fence.

At 4:30, the evening chores begin.

Careful feed rationing is important in order to maintain milk production.

The cattle are brought in from the field for evening milking.

Ralph tends the cattle as milking begins.

At five o'clock, Robert and Ransford start the evening milking.

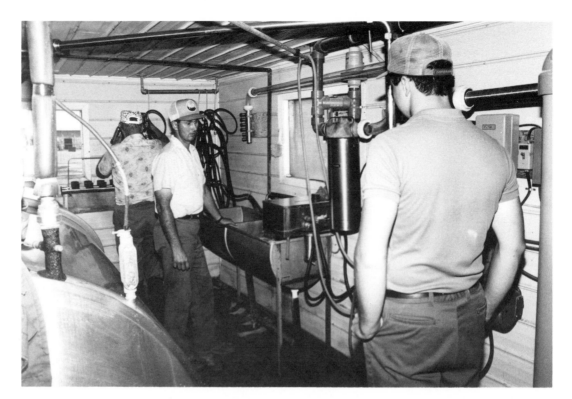

After milking, the clean-up begins.

A day-old calf requires special attention from David.

The men head in from the barn.

Marion prepares the evening meal.

After dinner, there's time to relax.

"...you've got to be efficient."

The weekday noon meal at the Streight's is like a Sunday-night feast. There's a roast of beef with gravy, fresh peas and potatoes, jugs of milk and fresh-baked, still-warm pie for dessert. Fifty-seven-year-old Marion has been cooking all morning in the summer kitchen. She's baked two pies — blueberry and chocolate — and a batch of butter tarts. Robert, Ransford, Ralph and David are hungry after six hours of farm work so they quickly settle down at their places around the oilcloth-covered table.

While Marion is getting the food on the table, the men go through the morning's mail. Robert opens the hydro bill, then rummages through an old pile of receipts.

"Here's a hydro bill from '65 and here's the one that came in the mail today," he says. "There's a big difference. In '65 it only cost twenty-eight dollars."

"The prices have changed a lot. In 1972 we paid five thousand and five hundred for a tractor. The same horsepower today would run you about thirty thousand."

"More like forty thousand," says his father, sixty-one-year-old Ransford. "You're talking big bucks on the farm."

The rising cost of farming is a constant source of conversation for farmers.

"You hear lots of bellyaching," comments Robert's uncle, sixty-five-year-old Ralph.

"C'est la vie," says Robert.

"I remember back years ago," says Ransford, "the cows would freshen about March or April or May and they'd milk them through until the fall and they'd dry them off. You didn't milk in the winter-time. But now you're milking year-round and you're shoving the cow for as much milk as you can get out of her and its called management."

"In the olden days," he continues, "everything was put down in salt, your pork and your beef, so you didn't buy much all winter. You more or less hibernated like a bear you see. You had no hydro to pay, you had no bills. You went to the store maybe once a month and that's all you'd ever go. Now, you've got costs coming in year-round and you've got to be efficient."

Right now, the farm is a three-way partnership between Robert, Ransford and Ralph. Robert and his wife Elizabeth, who works at Bell Northern Research in Ottawa, hope to take over some day. Robert says he couldn't imagine doing anything else.

"The secret to farming successfully," says Robert, "is you try to grow as much feed as you can on your own and buy the least amount from the feed store as possible. Then you can manage. You've got to get as much as possible out of each acre and each cow."

The men agree it's difficult for farmers just starting out. They say a quarter of a million dollars wouldn't go too far toward setting up a thirty-head dairy business. The milk quota alone would cost about two hundred thousand dollars.

Robert says that farmers brought the high price of quota on themselves because of their incessant demand for more. "As long as there's more that want to increase their size than want to decrease, then the price will keep going up and up. In 1980, pool one was seventy bucks, now we're looking at two forty-two."

33

Robert explains that every dairy farmer has a certain percentage of pool one, the higher-paying quota, and the rest is market-share quota, or MSQ as it's known to him. "Now don't get me wrong, both the MSQ and pool is the same milk and it goes in the same tank. One's for milk that goes into table milk, the MSQ goes into making butters, ice creams, yoghurts, et cetera. It's pretty complicated but it works."

The men finish their blueberry pie and head back to their fence work at one o'clock. They work for three and a half hours out in the fields putting new cedar posts in the ground, then it's milking time again.

"In the evening, we start milking at half past four," says Robert. "Ralph will clean the gutter of the dairy barn — it's cleaned twice a day, morning and night — and Dave and I will start

The Streights enjoy the family aspect of farming.

David takes time out for a little reading after a hard day's work.

putting the corn silage in. At five o'clock we start milking. Ralph's taking the manure to the field and then he starts putting in the hay for bedding. By six-thirty at the latest the hay's been thrown in and the cows are bedded down for the evening," says Robert.

But the Streights often visit the barn later in the evening.

"If a cow's going to freshen we go back and check during the night. I've seen times when a heifer or cow's going to freshen and you go back at eleven, you go back at one o'clock and she finally freshens around three which kind of ruins our night, but that's farming."

"Usually they do us a favour and do it in the daytime. Some people say, 'What the heck, let them freshen on their own', but it's better to be there. You can save the life of a heifer calf and they're worth money nowadays," says Robert.

"We're in big business nowadays. We're competing with all the manufacturers and plants. It's a business, it's not the way it used to be."

"There is a few dollars in farming, if you manage and watch yourself, but a lot of farmers' extra earnings at year-end get reinvested back into the farm, whereas people in an office put it into a savings plan," says Robert.

It's six-thirty, supper time. Robert, Ransford and Ralph go to their own homes on the farm. Aferwards, they may watch a bit of television and then they head off to bed early, ready for that 5 a.m. alarm.

To outsiders it may seem like a grueling way of life. There isn't much opportunity for a holiday and twelve-hour workdays are the norm. There's also the responsibility of the animals and the worry about what Mother Nature might deal them. But the Streights, like many other Ottawa Valley farmers, say they do it because they enjoy it. They take great pleasure in wandering through a field of towering corn, or seeing a healthy new-born calf. They also like the independence of farming and, above all else, they love their land: the back forty.

The family farm.

Chapter Two

I Farmed All My Life.

"Farmers are the kings of the world..."

There aren't many farmers that use a steam-powered threshing mill, but for Eric Campbell it's part of the fun of farming and he believes that farmers ought to have fun.

"When you take all the fun out of farming, what do you have left? Business and work, that's all farms are nowadays. I'm not making any money, but I'm having fun," says Eric as he surveys his one-hundred-and-fifty-acre farm in Clarendon, Quebec.

Eric says that he makes his fun by combining his hobbies with his livelihood. He likes old machines so he uses them on the farm. He's got a portable, seventeen-horse-power 1896 steam-engine which he uses to run a variety of equipment including his 2238 McCormick 1949 threshing- machine. He's also restoring an 1895 Sawyer and Massey steam tractor.

"I like the idea of running with wood. Steam was gone when I was a kid, but you would hear the

Eric collects steam-powered machinery.

Eric and Evelyn
Campbell

stories about it. I like the way the old machines were built. They're not making anything now that will be here in 2095 but these are eighty and a hundred years old and they're still working. Now that's something," says fifty-three-year-old Eric.

Others apparently share his interest. For years Eric and his forty-six-year-old wife Evelyn hosted a steam show which attracted upwards of three thousand people, but nowadays they're content with the hundred or so who show up when they hear the steam whistle blowing. "It gives me great pleasure to see all those people looking on," says Eric.

Eric is the first to admit that steam "thrashing," as he says it, is more work than a combine. Using steam, Eric has to cut the grain with a binder, stook it - arrange it into sheaves - then draw it to the threshing mill in the barnyard and fork it in. The modern way is to use a combine which does both the cutting and threshing, and puts the oats into a holding tank.

"Oh sure, it's more manual labour, but I like the old things. I've never combined, I've always thrashed." Eric threshes about nine hundred bushels of oats the last week of August each year to feed his cattle, horses and pigs.

In addition to steam machinery, Eric also collects tractors. He has three tractors on his farm at the moment, including the smallest-ever 1936 John Deere steel-wheeled tractor which is dwarfed by a 1955 model-55 Massey Harris Western Special.

Eric's infatuation with machinery began when he was just a child helping his father "thrash" for neighbours around the countryside. He was frustrated by the delays when equipment broke, and even back then he thought it would be better if he could repair his own equipment. His childhood dream has come true and today his machine-shop is crowded with some sixteen or so pieces of equipment including drills, welders, lathes, shapers, band-saws, shearers and milling machines. "I made that lathe there. I bought some machinery, in parts and pieces, and I bought some that needed to be rebuilt. Some I bought new," says Eric.

He taught himself how to repair every bit of machinery he owns, and if he can't find a part he just makes it. "If it's in metal, I can make it," he says. "I can make and do things you'd have trouble getting in Ottawa. For instance, I can cut spirals, I can make drill bits and gears."

It took three years of his spare time, but Eric built a portable sawmill for himself. He runs it with his portable steam-engine. "I've never seen one quite like it. It would probably cost about twenty-five thousand dollars to buy new." Eric uses the sawmill to make boards to repair his barns and sheds, and to make gates. He burns the leftover wood and bark in the steam-engine.

The sawmill, like all of Eric's farm equipment, is meticulously painted black with decorative yellow edging and curlicues. "I take pride in my work. That's something that's not found much any more. People are making things but they don't take pride in them," says Eric.

He gets many of his parts and pieces from auctions he attends around the countryside. "I don't throw out anything, I need it all," he says. He cautiously opens the door to a shed in the barnyard. It's filled, literally to the rafters, with bits and pieces of everything - chunks of fire-hose, belts, steam valves, pumps, pulleys and cans of grease. "I know where things are," Eric claims. "I sometimes have to dig a bit but I have my own computerized inventory, up here," says Eric, pointing to his head.

Eric's love for the traditional ways is also obvious in his choice of livestock. He has a truly old-fashioned mixed farm with a dozen pigs, ten Holsteins, eight or so Herefords and a horse. "The way I see it, you have to have a little of everything and then it don't matter about the market, whether it's good or bad. If you lose on the cows, you gain on the pigs, that's the way it goes," he says.

Evelyn and Eric enjoy traditional music.

He has a cream quota for his ten Holsteins and uses the skim milk to feed his pigs and calves. He doesn't milk in the winter. "I can't see the money in milking after the grass is gone. It just costs too much for feed. I'm lucky I can fill my quota in just the warm months," he says.

He runs a streamlined operation in the winter, only the Holsteins and horse remain; he sells his pigs and Herefords. "My pigs are sold now and they aren't even grown yet. There's always a good demand."

Eric, Evelyn and their nine-year-old daughter Vera-Lynn farm the same land that Eric's father farmed. Eric took over the farm when his dad died in 1959. Eric's not sure when his grandfather first settled on the farm. "I have a tax receipt here where the taxes were two dollars and a half in 1874."

Eric and Evelyn met while baling for a neighbour, and married in 1962. They also have a twenty-eight-year-old daughter, Betty-Lou. Today, Eric manages most of the farm business while Evelyn works as a registered nursing assistant at a senior citizens' home in nearby Shawville.

Eric also carries on the family tradition of making maple syrup. "I take a great interest in making syrup but I often thought dad made better syrup than I do." Eric used to tap five thousand trees in his bush, now he taps fifteen-hundred and produces about four hundred and fifty-five litres of maple syrup each year. He sells it all from the farm. "You make a bit of money but it's not easy money," he says.

Eric and Evelyn also make about seventy kilograms of maple sugar for their own use. "The best things in life are free - it just takes a bit of work," says Eric with a smile.

Amazingly, Eric and Evelyn also have time for a hobby. They play traditional music with neighbours Betty Cameron and Basil Hodgins. As would be expected, Eric taught himself to play the fiddle. His wife plays guitar. Eric denies that the group is a band. "We just get together to play music. There's no name, nothing ever got that far." The group plays at dances and parties and has also put together three tapes entitled Old Time Country, Favourite Fiddle Tunes, and Fiddlers of the Past.

"We try to keep alive some of the old traditional music of the area," he says. "It's part of our heritage and part of our culture. I don't want it to be forgotten."

Eric says that with his music, his farm, his machining, and his syrup, "I'm never bored and I'm never short of work. I like a mix up, I don't like one thing better than another. I need a lot of things to keep my attention."

Eric is obviously very proud to be a farmer. "Farmers are the kings of the world, always will be, always have been since the beginning of time. What do you eat if there's no farmers?"

Eric says that it upsets him to see farms around his closing down. "There are too many auctions; too many are leaving." He says that what the modern farm really needs is a good dollop of old-fashioned, neighbourly co-operation. "There's only one solution and that's getting together and working together. Don't work with a big mortgage, work with your neighbour; share time, help and equipment," says Eric.

But then he admits that that sort of co-operation just isn't too likely to happen these days. "That goes against the grain of the government. They don't want you to do that anymore. It's like a barter system and the government can't tax that."

So, instead of depending on the bank's money or neighbourly kindness to help make his farm succeed, Eric depends on his impressive metal machining skills, a wide variety of farm products and a pay-as-you-go philosophy. But the thing that helps him make it all worthwhile is his attitude: "We're likely only making one trip through, we're not going to get a rerun so you've got to do what you want."

Eric on his way to the barns.

Lorne gets ready to work in the fields.

"...you feel like doing the best you can."

Lorne Siegel, Rankin

"I married my wife in 1939 and we took the farm over. It was my wife's parents'. At that time it was tough going; you couldn't make a cent. You couldn't sell a log, you couldn't sell cattle. Ten dollars for two-year-old steers. I took the farm over and they had two steers and Vern Risto come along and he said, 'I'd like to buy those steers.' And I said, 'That's fine.' I said I wanted twenty dollars a piece for them and he went around them again and looked at them and he said, 'I can't pay you that.' 'Well,' I said, 'You better leave then, they'll get bigger and when they get bigger maybe they'll be worth a little more.' So he went around them again and looked at them and he said, 'I'd like to have

those two steers.' And I said, 'I'm just starting up on the farm, I need to make some money to pay off the farm.' So he wandered around them again and he said, 'Okay, I'll take them for twenty dollars a piece.' He said, 'I know I'm going to lose on them.' 'Well,' I said, 'Don't take them if you lose, leave them here.' But he took them anyway. That's the way it started.

"I was working in the mines before I got married and in the winter-time we were sitting here with her parents and my wife and I said we can't do nothing here. I said, 'How can we make a living, how can we have a decent life?' I said, 'Wouldn't it be all right if I'd go back to the mine again and you just keep the thing living and feed the cattle?' They didn't have many. I said, 'Lets think it over. Tomorrow we'll talk more about it.' So we did too, and her dad said, 'Do you think you can get back on?' I said there was no problem. So then I packed up everything and the next day I went to Sudbury. I stayed there for three years and things were looking a little better and her parents were getting a little older and they found it harder. That winter my wife came up and stayed with me and they were here all alone and I guess they found it lonesome too and so they wrote us a letter and said, 'You better come home and look after the farm.' And so I said, 'Okay Edith, we'll go home.' And so we went back and started farming.

"The farm was lacking in everything, like fertilizer. So I went on one field and I said to the wife, 'I'm going to put one field in shape as good as I know how.' So I plowed it, put fertilizer on it all and next spring I seeded it with oats and with grass seed and boy I had a catch the next year. And then her father came along and he came over here when I was cutting hay and there was red clover. I seeded everything from broom grass to alfalfa and red clover and white clover but red clover is the one that caught. So he walked over there and had a look and he said, 'One thing, my son, I must say you know how to farm.' That's what he told me. I was brought up on a farm and you feel like doing the best you can. Now I'm seventy-seven years of age and I go and cut hay and rake and everything and if I don't do that I don't feel good."

Edith and Lorne Siegel

Bob looks out over the Ottawa River.

"There was nine of us in the family..."

Bob and Doris Ferguson, Castleford

"No one has ever lived here by any other name. The Depression was the toughest time of all. There was nine of us in the family and that was tough going; there wasn't any money. I worked in the bush in the winter-time and my dad and grandfather worked in the bush in the winter-time. They'd take the horses and go to the bush. That was the way a lot of the farmers done it then. That was more before the Depression. The Depression came and you couldn't get a job in the bush. And this wasn't the worst part of the world either; where Doris came from was worse than here. Doris was raised in Saskatchewan.

They couldn't grow anything. They'd plant a crop and then the wind would come and blow it away and the topsoil along with it. I went west in the late '30s on a harvest excursion. There was three of us that went out there and we got a job all right; there was a bit of a crop that year."

"He came to where I was working. I was cooking for a bachelor that had hired help and he was on the farm right next to us. I was cutting hair for everybody around there and these guys needed a haircut and the barbershop was closed in Riverhurst so they sent them over to me and so that's how we got started. I've been cutting hair ever since. We got married out west fifty years ago this fall. We had two weddings really; out west we had one with my family and we came down here and your mother had made another wedding cake and the family was all here and then the neighbours all came in."

Doris and Bob Ferguson

"I was used to the bush and there was no bush out there and water was scarce too. The first trip we went out we had an old '34 Pontiac convertible coupe. You couldn't go the whole way in Canada then; there was no road from Soo to Port Arthur and so we crossed over at the Soo into the States and we ducked back into Canada at International Falls and they told us there was a road from there up to Kenora. We got through up to Kenora but before we got to Winnipeg the piston went out of the car. So we walked for a piece and came to a service station and borrowed some tools and got a used piston and a used connecting-rod and went back and put them in. It didn't take us very long to do. We went right through then to Swift Current. Doris has worked on the farm ever since she came here."

"I drove tractors and horses. For a while we milked twenty-five cows by hand. We started off with a milking machine but they were Durham cattle and they weren't built for milking machines. We had short-horned cattle then but as soon as we found out that at the sale barns white faces could get you five cents a pound more we switched and brought in a white-faced bull. And that's what we've been doing ever since."

Bob walks the fields.

Aileen and Joe Dellaire

"It was a stony place."

Joe Dellaire, Eganville

"I got married in 1930 and I bought my dad's place. It was a mixed farm. It was a stony place. My first wife died in September of '33 and I married Aileen in August of '35. We quit farming in '68. We quit because there was only the two of us, and we had six cottages on Constant Lake where White Cedars is now. I cut the hay in the fields where the cottages were and then they could come in and pitch a tent and do whatever they wanted. We got thirty dollars a week for a cottage and Aileen furnished the bedding. And then we put it up to thirty-five when the electricity came in. After we retired, I didn't miss farming, I missed the cattle and the horses, but we didn't miss the work a damn bit. We missed the people coming to the cottages, that we missed. We couldn't wait till spring, until they started to come.

"We'll be married fifty-five years in August. We got married in Griffith at seven o'clock in the morning. We were supposed to go on down to Pakenham and catch the train at Hyndford at eight-thirty or nine o'clock. But the guy that was supposed to look after the place while we were gone, he got a job and so we couldn't go."

Harry and Lors Brownlee

"And there's a seat on the tractor..."

Harry and Lors Brownlee, Clarendon

"Our father bought this farm in 1888. It was mostly cleared and he cleared some and stumped some. It was a hundred acres when he bought it and I guess they added thirty acres to it and then added another hundred to it and Lors bought another hundred and fifty. Altogether there's three hundred and eighty acres. It's all beef cattle. We had dairy and we switched over to beef because we thought it would be easier just to feed the cows than to milk them. I think the tractor is a lot easier. You used to come in at night and you'd unharness your horses and feed them and clean them up, that takes quite a little while. You come in on a tractor and you just get off it. And there's a seat on the tractor; there wasn't with the horses. We got our first tractor in '48. We started in with a Cockshutt 70.

"I remember when the phones came in. I remember the fellow who was putting them in staying here over night. He put in Hodgin's phone over there and then he came over here and put ours in and stayed over night here. We called them up, after we got the phone in, to see if it was working. I thought that was quite a thing. We paid sixty dollars to start with, to get the phone, and then six dollars, twice a year, for service. It was something in them days too. My father tells the story of being at the flour mill and getting some wheat ground and they got to talking there about the phone. One fellow stepped up and said you just take a thing in your hand and say, 'What's the price of eggs in Montreal?' And you find out; they'll tell you what the price of eggs is in Montreal. That was unbelievable you know, to think that you could do that."

Harry and Lors relax in their kitchen.

Wilmer Campbell

"I pretty nearly cry now when I think about how hard I worked my horses..."

Wilmer Campbell, Ashton

"There's not too many staying too interested in farming because there's too much work for the money that's in it. The only way you can get rich farming is by selling the farm. I farmed the other side of the town line here. My dad bought the farm over there when I was three years old. I think I was born in Ramsay, in either Huntley or Ramsay. My dad was in Ramsay when he got married first. I think he went to Carleton Place and then he came out on a farm in Ramsay and then he went to another farm in Huntley. When I was three years old he bought this farm over in Beckwith and then he and I kind of farmed together till I got married in 1928. Then I rented a farm in Goulbourn, a hundred and forty dollars a year for fifty acres and a house to live in. I was there for four years then I went back up to my dad's.

"I bought a lot of different farms. I started out differently than people did before that. All around here, when somebody was born on the farm and their dad died, it went to the son and the son worked on that farm. He never went across the road to rent a field or he never rented another farm; he just lived on that farm and everybody seemed to do the same thing. But I didn't do that, I just started to reach out. I never had any money to buy a farm but I'd pay for it after. I'd go to auction sales and I'd buy cattle. I was a younger fellow then and the older fellows would wonder what the heck I would do with them. Some of those cattle I'd sell before I'd left the sale. I'd make a profit, but not a great big profit.

"I don't know what to think of the farmers today. I think you just got to love farming to be farming today. Farming has changed a lot. You couldn't farm today like you used to farm. You've got to have money. It's not near as neighbourly any more. Years ago you were back and forth with your neighbours; you'd buy a calf from your neighbour or you'd sell him a couple of pigs and back and forth like this. There's none of that now.

"I had some awful good horses. I pretty nearly cry now when I think about how hard I worked my horses to try and make a living. I had a team, the best horses in this part of the country, and they got old like I have. I'd go out to sow a field of grain and come around four o'clock I'd still have a half an hours work to do and those horses, one of them especially, when you went up the side of his front leg he went like this with weakness. But I wanted to get that other few rounds there to finish the field. I wouldn't do it now. If the field was never sowed, I wouldn't do it. It was work long hours and work hard. At that time I could do it, but now I can't. I go to the bush now.

"When we were first married, for a long time, we never took any pleasure, dances or socials or anything else, because you couldn't afford to go. We just didn't have the money. We lived for the first four years on the other side of Ashton here and on the night of the social we could hear the music. We both liked music and we both liked dancing but it was twenty-five or thirty-five cents to get in and we just didn't have the money. It just took every last cent that you had to keep from going under. About the second year we

Wilmer at his kitchen table.

were farming we killed four pigs and my brother-in-law had a car and we put them in the car and went to Ottawa with them to sell them on the market. We brought them home again; all they would give us was three and a half cents a pound, for dressed meat. I sold them between Carp and Ottawa for four cents a pound. You'd only get six or eight dollars for a pig that weighed a hundred pounds. It pretty near cost you more than you got for it. There's nothing else I like better than farming. I was able to buy farms and sell them and I got up to pretty well the top of the ladder but it was a long time down on the bottom step."

"...we started to farm on seventeen dollars..."

Norval McNeill, Charteris

"We bought this place from my mother in 1935 and we started to farm here. There was two hundred and sixty acres and we started to farm on seventeen dollars with a team of horses and a buggy and a plow and a mowin' machine and ten sheep and twenty-five hens. Lambs were worth about two dollars and a half, a piece at that time, and eggs was eight cents a dozen. Butter fat was fourteen cents a pound. We kept ourselves that summer on butter and milk, and we had six dollars and ninety-five cents in a cheque from the creamery in the fall. And I cut pulpwood at two dollars and a half a cord and piled it on the side of the road, and at haying time I took off the hay. In '35 we had no wagon and the Frostt and Wood agent came along here

Norval McNeill is renowned locally for his fiddle playing.

to sell a wagon. Billy Dagg was the head agent for the Frostt and Wood Company. So anyway, he drove into the yard here and he said, 'I understand you have no wagon.' And I said, 'No.' 'Well,' he said 'what kind of a wagon would you want to buy if you were buying a wagon?' 'Well,' I said, 'at the present time I wouldn't want to buy any wagon at any price because I have no money.' He just handed me the catalogue. 'Well,' he said, 'if you were buying a wagon what kind of a wagon would you buy?' 'Well,' I said, 'if I was buying a wagon I'd buy that number fifty-two...' 'Well,' he said, 'that will be here next week for you.' 'Well,' I said, 'I have no money,' and he said, 'Never mind, that will be here next week for you. We're not looking for money, we're looking to sell you a wagon that you'll have comfort on the farm for the summer, to go ahead and work.' So anyway the next week our neighbour came and told us here — we had no phone — and he said the wagon was at Shawville. So the wife and I hitched up the team and the buggy and we went to Shawville and we tied the buggy behind the wagon and we brought it home. I made a rack for it and set to work with it. Then came the harvest. We got my father's binder and we got the harvest off that year and we got it threshed and the next year I bought an old binder from Bert Kirkham for eight dollars.

So anyways we started on from that then, and we got more cattle and we had more sheep and we had thirty-three ewes at one time here and we had over forty lambs. I guess it was in 1948 that the wolf got into them and killed twelve in the one night. So anyway we kept them in at night for a couple of years and then we had to sell them.

"People don't work the same today as they did back then. I could put up two cord of pulpwood every day, with a Swede, cut right at the stump and limb it and pile it up. Two cord every day. I say they're doing it with a chain-saw now and they're not putting up the wood that we done in our day. We cut a hundred and twenty-five logs a day."

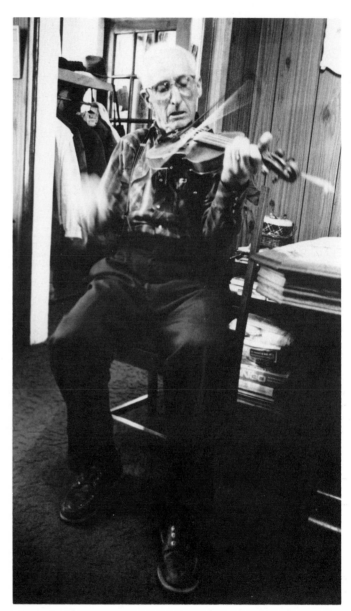

Norval plays a tune.

Norval McNeill

"I've seen us threshing through Christmas..."

Emery Smith, Stittsville

"I was raised on fried pork and fried potatoes three times a day. Then when I was ten years old my grandma passed away and mother came on as cook and we got into porridge and stuff like that. I was raised on the farm up there and then dad bought this farm in '29. There was just a little house and a hay barn and that's all there was on it. This farm here was owned by the O'Grady people but they lived over where Hammills lived and this was their second farm, you see. They took a notion to either rent or sell this place, so we took a notion. I was just out of school — I only got my grade eight — and we decided to buy it, eight thousand dollars. A dollar more or a dollar less wouldn't buy it; that was the price. We bought it and along came the Depression and cattle dropped down to fifteen dollars a piece. So we had ten years of very tough times.

"My father had a steam-engine that had the smoke-stack on the back end instead of the front end. I grew up with that. I've seen us threshing through Christmas and New Year's. My father used to have to get up through the night and put

Emery and Emily Smith

58

Emery is proud of his steam-engine.

a fire on in the engine to keep it warm. I can remember when I was going to school everybody barn threshed. You put the stacks up in August; by the time it comes November it's getting pretty soggy. They'd come around, threshing stacks first and they'd go away for a while and they'd come back around December and the farmers would have their plowing done. The farmers didn't want to see them till they got their plowing done and when they got their plowing done they were freer. In the evening you threshed till dark; you should have seen the fire come out of the engine at night, blowing sparks. It was the same all day but you didn't see them. We burned wood mostly but father used to go over to Twin Elm here and coal was five dollars a ton and he'd get a wagon load and that would thresh maybe three days. It would come in lumps and I can remember we used to crack them with the axe. There was several barns burned from threshing-machines. We carried a quarter-inch mesh screen and we put it in the smoke-stack. Of course the engine fired much nicer without the screen. Then the tractors came in and steam tractors were shoved to one side and along came World War number II and scrap dealers got them for fifty dollars. I'm all for the new stuff; them days have passed now."

59

"You had enough to eat and lots of wood to keep you warm."

Wesley and Mina Dagg, Shawville

"I enjoyed farming. We called it a family farm in those days and we had a little bit of everything. We didn't specialize in anything and that's the way most of the farming was done around here in the '30s and '40s. You had enough to eat and lots of wood to keep you warm."

"I was born here and when my parents went out west and both died, my grandparents raised us. My grandfather was a minister and eventually, after much travelling, we landed at Foresters Falls. My grandmother died there and after a few months I decided to come over to my mother's people. My mother's sister was married to Wesley's older brother. We were good friends for five years and then we decided to take the final step. I've stayed with him for fifty-eight years, it'll be fifty-nine in September.

"When we were living up here the Farm Forum came along and that was a great thing for the country people. We met in different homes once a week and there was a radio discussion that was broadcasted from McDonald College concerning different trends in farming. That was very strong around here. I don't know how many different groups there were in the area. We discussed whatever the broadcast was about. There'd be a sheet that would come through the mail ahead of time with questions to get our opinions on these topics. After the meeting we played cards or had a lunch. It was very casual and very relaxing. We took our kids with us when we went in the winter in a sleigh. We'd gather up everybody close and we had quilts or buffalo rugs or whatever we could find to cover us. I think we learned quite a bit from it and one of the biggest things I guess is it brought the community together. At Christmas we'd have a party and we often drew names and exchanged gifts. If the meeting was to be at one of the bigger homes or if somebody volunteered we had a dance a few times."

"I worked in the bush here. There was one time, during the Depression, when a farmer up the road here was about to lose his farm, and a neighbour took on the job of cutting his bush out. He had a lot of bush and I forget just what the arrangement was but I think it was we'd cut everything on about six acres. It was mostly pine and poplar. The man that was selling the bush got fifty cents a cord and he paid us and he got enough money to hold on to his farm. We would've been further ahead to have sat doing nothing. All we got was the clothes we wore. You certainly didn't make any money at all but it was something to do. I didn't have so much fun; I was home doing the chores."

Mina and Wesley Dagg

Donald Farquharson

"I've always had chickens."

Donald Farquharson, Renfrew

"We've lived here since '51. We were always into poultry. We started off with a hatching flock and sold the eggs to a hatchery in Renfrew. That went on for a few years, then we got into a big flock of broilers. That year we had quite a few of them and the bottom went right out. We were left with all of these birds and we were feeding them and the eggs were worth nothing. So we killed them all and we went into the laying hens. We used to have about three thousand out on the range which is not a big amount compared to what they're doing now. I had a contract with the hospital in town and some other outlets and we were at that for quite a few years. Then it got to the point where you had to go into cages and go bigger to have any income and so we decided it wasn't worth it. The kids were all leaving home. I always kept about four or five hundred heavy meat birds and I got the equipment from The Co-operators down here; they used to have a killing plant down there just outside of Renfrew, and I did custom killing.

"I had a few birds when I was growing up. I've always had chickens. It's something you can get into in a small way at the start and work up. I always bought the day-old chicks and then raised them up. If you have the place it's a little cheaper.

"There's not too many birds around here anymore; there's just a few small flocks. It's a lot of work, poultry. I've never been leery about getting into something but you've got to have enough to make a living, and if you get too much stuff you just run yourself ragged."

Looking out the back door of Donald's house.

"And so I had to cut down..."

Alex Russell, Shawville

"My farm was one of the first places settled in this area right around through here. The barn was built around 1918 by David Thompson and he died, I think sometime in the '30s and he never was married. There was a fellow held a mortgage on it and dad bought it from him. They say the farm's two hundred and fifty acres and there's about a hundred and fifty that's workable and the rest is bush and swamp. I have beef cattle and we used to have dairy cattle and we had hens and pigs, horses. You had to buy the feed for the hens and the pigs and the help too. I had hired help for a few years but I was working for them, so I got rid of them and worked for myself. They were taking everything that was coming in. The day you wanted them they wouldn't be here and you'd have to roll up your sleeves and do two men's work. So I said what I could do myself I'd do, and what I couldn't, I'd just leave it alone. And so I had to cut down on the pigs and the hens. I'm kind of half-retired now. The

Alex finds time to relax.

Alex Russell

neighbours cut the hay and bale it. In July, I start to get the pension.

"I remember dad saying he sold twenty-one head of cattle for two hundred and ten dollars and he sold a team of horses for a hundred and seventy-five. This was during the Depression. There was one lad was supposed to ship some sheep and the railroad said the sheep didn't bring enough to pay the freight and so they sent him a bill and he wrote back and he said he didn't have no money but he had more sheep.

"There was no hired help in the townships then and so each year, each farmer had so many days what they called road-work. You could either pay or do it and nobody had any money so you went and you done it. There'd be what they would call a road foreman and he was just another farmer, and council would appoint him and he'd tell you to bring the horses or an axe or a shovel."

Alex in his living-room.

"...I wouldn't mind doing the whole thing again."

Henry Pacquette, Perrault

"I started farming with my father. I got married in '39 and I farmed till about 1950. Not altogether just farming. I built up that building there, that blacksmith shop, for shoeing horses and machinery repairs and stuff like that. I didn't have any more than eight cows here, and fifty sheep and a team of horses. You wouldn't have been able to work this land here with a tractor at that time, it was all rock. I started to blacksmith because I had to do some of my own repairs and I couldn't afford to pay for them and so I started to do mine and then I had everybody else's. And then, as it changed, the rubber wagons started to come out and I had to build the rubber-tired wagons out of old cars or trucks. And so then, eventually, the horses went out and it came time for the tractors. I shoed horses in the lumber camps and I built sleighs too. It has been about twenty years since I shoed my last horse. You'd start shoeing a team of horses here after supper and sometimes you'd have to make all new shoes and if they had bad feet it would take you to twelve o'clock to finish off. A farmer would come here with a team of horses. They already had some shoes and so you'd renew the shoes and cork them, refit them and trim their feet, and all you'd charge them was twenty-five dollars to renew them. I really enjoyed my work, really, if I was young again and I was able as I was, I wouldn't mind doing the whole thing again."

Frances and Henry Pacquette

Carmen Wickens

"I've been here ever since I was born."

Carmen Wickens, Clarendon

"My father bought this farm from Bob Storey. At that time everybody had a half a dozen cows and they made a little butter. I've been here ever since I was born. I had milk and beef both, until three years ago, and then I quit milking and so I have just beef now. I had some pigs too and I got rid of the last one last month. There's no money in pigs now. Up until last fall I had about two hundred and fifty cows and I have a hundred and fifty now. We have four hundred acres here and then I rent some land too. The odd time I have some help. I have a son who works for the Ottawa Board of Education and he comes up and cultivates on the weekends. Last summer I sort of took a holiday. I had a back operation and the neighbours did quite a bit. I had quite a few help with the hay when I was in the hospital. My father was here till he died. In '52 I rented the farm from him and that's when I started buying machinery. He died in '59."

Clelland and Ruby Hamilton

"We were driving up around the telephone wires."

Clelland and Ruby Hamilton, Russell

"We bought this farm in 19 and 35. My home was right at the next farm and I grew up there. This farm was for sale and my father bought it. The house was the only good building on the farm because the barn only held ten cows. There was a barn over in the field over there that had been built twenty-five or thirty years before and it was a good barn. It was thirty-six by forty-eight and they used it for hay. We moved that barn over about three years after we were married I guess. That was a chore in those days. We hired people to come and move it in the winter-time. They jacked it up and put sleighs under it and drew it with a winch. There was a horse going around in a circle here winding up the winch. When we were married we moved here right away."

"I lived next farm to him. He had seven cows when we got married and my dad gave me two and so we had nine and he gave us a dozen pullets. We had just two horses when we started to work all this land. I remember that fall he was plowing this field with a one-furrow plow. And then he'd walk up and down behind the harrows and the big chunks he'd have to walk over."

"When we moved that barn over here we made it a stable right through and then we could tie up about forty cows. Since then we've built another barn which is sixty by a hundred so now we're milking about thirty-five but we have about a hundred head in there altogether. Our son bought the farm from us about five years ago; of course I help him but he owns the farm.

"I went to high school for two years but I wasn't interested in doing anything else but farming. My father needed help then and I stayed home."

"When he stayed home he started to work long hours and he is still today and he'll be seventy-seven this fall. You can't retire and live on a farm. He gets up at five-thirty and he's not in for breakfast till eight-thirty, there's three hours of chores. At night in the summer we have lots to do outside. So we've been quite a team."

"I made a tractor from the front part of a '28 Chev car and in those days there was a company that made the pinion and the wheels and the gears for the back end. You could buy it as a kit and I bought one in Ottawa and I used it for five or six years. It had steel lugs on it. I brought it out on a sleigh. My father and I went into Ottawa on the fourteenth of March. My father used to sell grass seed a lot, timothy seed, and he had two tons he wanted to sell so he went into Ritchie's to see if they would buy it and they wanted to and I went in to see about the tractor. Then on a Saturday it started to storm and the train couldn't leave till the next Thursday. All the roads were blocked up all over the place. So my father and I took the team and sleigh and put on the two tons of grass seed and drove into Ottawa to Ritchie's and unloaded it. We put the tractor on the sleigh and we came up the hill here at Bronson Avenue and right to Heron Road and went across Heron Road. We were driving up around the telephone wires."

A proud married couple.

"He was the first person who ever sold milk door-to-door in Arnprior..."

Tom Havey, Arnprior

"I've been seventy-three years here. I'm not farming much now; I don't have much land left. Originally we had two hundred and forty-five acres here. Then, during the war, the airport bought the upper hundred plus twenty some acres off the side. Since then the hydro built this dam and they flooded some of our land and that took another chunk off. We still farm though, and when I say we it's mostly my son Jim. We've been in the dairy business for years. My grandfather farmed right here. He was the first person who ever sold milk door-to-door in Arnprior; up to that time everybody or every second house along the street had a cow. He started peddling milk and it wasn't even bottled. They used to have cans and you pulled the lid off and it served as a measure and you poured the milk out into a bowl or something that the lady had. This was when my father was a young fellow. I remember the old cans. They held about three gallons and they weren't even galvanized in those days. I don't know how they kept them clean. They peddled milk like that for years and they finally got a contract. They sold milk and shipped it by train every day down to Ottawa to Producer's Dairy. You'd have a single horse and you'd go down to the station every morning with the milk cans.

"They had a cheese factory up the road here a couple of miles and I can remember one summer taking milk up to the cheese factory. We had eight-gallon cans, that's eighty pounds, and we used to get eighty cents a can. There was one month, it was the month of June, and we had a high milk production and we got almost a two hundred dollar cheque for the month. That was the talk of the whole neighbourhood: 'Havey's got two hundred dollars this month.' That wasan awful pile of money. That was in the mid '30s.

"My grandfather and another man were in partnership. They would buy five hundred acres from the Crown and they'd hire some men to go in there and they'd build sort of a shanty type of house and a stable for the horses and they'd start cutting all the stuff off it. They sold the logs and the pulp and that kind of thing and they burned all the brush. Then, in the spring when the frost came out of the ground, they'd use these stumping machines and take all the stumps out and clear that farm and then they'd sell it to some farmer. There was already a place for the farmer to live and there was a place for his livestock. So they sold the place and then they'd move on to the next farm. They cleared an awful pile of land and they made money at it but it must of been tedious work.

"What I miss most is when I quit milking cows. I was a whole year getting over that. Every morning at half past five I was awake. It was in my blood; I had done it for years and years."

Tom Havey

Russell Comba

"I was the last one to quit."

Russell Comba, White Lake

"I was born here. It's been in my family way over a hundred years. I farmed all the time. They used to farm just to make a living. I used to have cattle and sheep and pigs. I quit because of my heart. It was disappointing when you had to quit all of a sudden. When you don't want to and have to, it's a different thing.

"This place grew a lot of stuff. We had a few good years and a few good crops. Mother was here till she died. They used to work long hours and hard hours. There are no farms around here at all; they all quit. I was the last one to quit. If I was young again, I'd do the same thing over; I enjoyed it. You had your own hours, and you were your own boss. I took over the farm once dad got unable to. My dad was a good farmer. We got up at five o'clock every morning and went to bed maybe at ten o'clock. You got used to them hours.

Russell warms up by his wood stove.

The front hall.

"You were up through the winter, at night, calving; maybe you were up half the night or all night with a cow coming in. I've taken a lot of calves. If the leg was turned back that she couldn't calf, you'd have to shove the calf back and shove your hand in and get the leg and pull it out. You take all your clothes off and you put your hand in up to here often. I've done that a few times. I done that one night at twenty below zero out in an old, open shed of my neighbour's. Darn near froze. I got the calf, it lived but the cow wouldn't lick it, so we gave it a good old rubbing and got the circulation through it and pulled it up beside the cow. I remember the first one I did, I had to do it, that was all there was to it, and I had seen dad at it all the time. He showed me a lot of what to do. The first one I got with no trouble. There was only one I had to call the vet; the leg was back, and I just couldn't get it out."

Florence and Wilbert Munro

"If I was starting back today, I'd farm just the same way."

Wilbert Munro, Clayton

"I started to farm here with my dad. I was the youngest in the family. We started to draw wood to town and I drew wood to Almonte for twenty-two years and we farmed in the summer. We'd draw wood to where the IGA is now in Almonte. They'd park maybe thirty or forty teams in there and you waited till one o'clock to see if somebody would come and buy the load and then, if they didn't, you called in every house along the road to see if you could sell it. In them times we milked about twelve cows and there was a cheese factory in Clayton and the milkman would pick up the milk at six o'clock in the morning. We kept five horses and we worked three horses together. In 1934, we were married. In '34, Florence and I took two veal calves to Carleton Place and we sold them for two cents a pound. If I was starting back today, I'd farm just the same way. Florence worked on the farm and she worked in the bush as well as any man. She could handle a Swede saw far better than lots of men I hired. We never had a baby-sitter in our life, we took the children with us."

Wilbert in the summer kitchen.

"There was a cheese factory on every corner."

Wendell Stanley, Russell

"My grandfather bought this piece of land in 1867. My dad was born in this house and I was born in this house. I started to farm here when I was about eighteen. My dad got sick my last year of school. I wanted to go to school but at that time there wasn't money and so what could you do? So, I stayed at home on the farm.

"It was during the Depression. We had a dairy farm, a general dairy farm, and went to the cheese factory. Everybody at one time practically went to cheese factories in this part of eastern Ontario. There was a cheese factory on every corner. There was one on the back end of our farm and it was very handy. When you were working back there, you could have an excuse to rest the horses and you could go in and see if they had any curd to eat. And then there was another cheese factory just up the road here, about a quarter of a mile, which was closer than the one at the back end so we went to the other one. This area was all dairy cattle, nobody had beef cattle. The farms were all pretty good for farming; there wasn't any bush or rough land and it was pretty well tillable so you could make more money, I suppose, with twenty milk cows than you could with twenty beef cattle. It was a different world altogether then. As a rule the cheese factory was closed early December or late November, so you'd have a rest all winter. You didn't have to milk too much, you had a few cows and you had one cow anyway you called her a stripper. She'd be for milk in the house. She'd be the one that wouldn't freshen until very, very late in the summer and so she'd milk over the winter.

"There was an awful uproar when they started to talk about running the cheese factories on Sundays; after all, no good Christian should be taking milk to the factory on Sunday. You'd never catch anybody working out in the fields on Sunday with horses or anything like that, it just wasn't done, no matter what. The horse got a rest on Sunday unless they took him to church.

"I used to do the factory books for the patrons. I'd issue the cheques and figure out how much money each one got. There were about thirty-five patrons at that time and I got eighty-five cents a piece, so you know how much money I got for a year's work. When you went in, in the morning, the cheese maker marked down how much cheese you had on a sheet of paper. At the end of the month the inspector would give me the figures and what the cheese sold for and then I had to figure out what each farmer got for his milk. I kept at it till the factory went out of business.

"In '59 I ran into a health problem and had to give up farming and in the spring of '60 there was an opening came in the registry office and that's where I worked for twenty-two years; I was the land registrar in Russell."

Wendell in his younger days.

Wendell Stanley

"We were getting fifty cents a dozen..."

Don Miller, Carleton Place

"I had never even been on a farm other than working on one for a couple of summers. I didn't want to become involved in industry and I ended up talking to the war veteran's land-act people about maybe buying farm property. So we ended up buying a one-hundred-and-fifty-acre farm with a stone house and barns. By that time we had three small children. The mistake we made in the farming wasn't the farm we bought, the farm was quite good, but we stocked it with pure-bred jerseys and this isn't a jersey area. Lanark County is Holstein. It went not too badly for us simply because at that time Elsie the Borden cow and trade-mark jersey milk was at a premium and you could sell every jersey that you could get your hands on. It was a market that was world-wide. Practically every herd had a jersey. One lonesome jersey in a herd of maybe twenty-five Holsteins to bring up the high-test milk.

"I had an air force injury and it started coming back on me. I guess in about '67 I was in a cast for eleven months and it was extremely difficult to operate a farm from a cast, so we started changing and going heavier into pure-bred Herefords. Of course we were growing cash crops such as wheat too. When the last jersey went out the gate I was kind of sorry because most of them by that time we had raised ourselves. We still get Herefords in the summer.

"When we started farming you didn't seem to need money. You were lucky if you had a light hanging in the middle of the kitchen let alone having lights in your barns. When I first started out, I bought my animals and moved the last one into the barn at nine o'clock at night. I had no money left but at a quarter to seven in the morning I was putting cans of milk on the milk stand to go to the dairy in Almonte. We were in business and your milk cheque brought you a steady money. My father owned and operated the hotel in Carleton Place and he gave us an egg contract; he wanted fifty dozen at a time and he'd pay a flat rate. We were getting fifty cents a dozen across the board for the eggs. At the same time we had a contract with the little store at the corner. It had just started and they said, 'We'll take all the eggs you can give us.' So we would pile them sky-high on Saturday afternoons and they would sell them to the campers on the way back to Ottawa."

Don Miller

Lloyd Streight

"I got along the best I could."

Lloyd Streight, Kemptville

"Everybody said, 'Sell all the cattle, sell all the cattle and quit.' It's nice not to have any cattle but, still in all, you can't run around the road every day; you might as well be doing a little bit of work at home, and the cattle will make you a dollar or so. I bought this farm in 1944. I was up there at my brother's, my father was running it then, and he didn't need me very bad, so Tim Findlay from Manotick came up and hired me, and I was down there for over two years. This was a good little place to buy. It was a good location and a good road and everything like that, and that's why I bought it. Tim Findlay said, 'The road's worth a thousand dollars to you.' And so I bought it. I haven't been sorry at all, except I haven't made a whole lot of money out of it. I had milk cows up till '77, and then I sold them and got into beef cattle. I changed because I didn't want to go into bulk. We were shipping milk in cans, and they were going to have to change, in the fall, to bulk tanks in the milk house, and I didn't want to go to that expense because I wasn't a big enough farmer, eh. I got along the best I could. I'm old enough for the pension."

An old-fashioned farm house.

Lloyd prepares to do some work in the barn.

"...I guess it took less money to survive."

Edgar Pilatzke, Eganville

"I plow and sand the roads in the winter. In '58 I started on the snow, I always liked the snow removal. I had a kind of a liking to see the snow roll and in them years it was severe and the fences used to be buried. But I'm getting older and I couldn't hack it anymore.

"This place is my homestead. I used to have twenty-five, thirty sheep, twenty-five cows. I cut off the sheep about ten years ago and three years ago I parted with the cows. But we still cut hay and we sell it off the fields and we do a bit of cropping. We still have chickens and we get in a few pigs for the summer too. We used to salt hams. We used to put them in brine and then smoke them. I still smoke sausages.

"My father had a bit of a blacksmith shop and he'd do a lot of the repair work on his own and he'd fix up the horseshoes. He could weld iron just by heating it and he'd make these rings for the end of whippletrees and neck yokes and axe handles. Now it seems to be too fast and you just don't have the time to do all that stuff. Years ago they seemed to have more time; they got less money but I guess it took less money to survive. I guess when cars were invented that's when you stopped talking to your neighbour. I know years ago, when I was young, my father would go to town and you would think nothing of it if you met your neighbour you just stopped and had a chat; today you don't have time, you're lucky if you give them a wave."

Edgar still keeps a few chickens and other livestock.

Edgar Pilatzke

"There was lots of stones."

Jack King, Clayton

"I was born here in 1909. There was ten in the family I was in. Two died and eight lived and I'm the last. On Sunday they caught you by the hand and you went to Sunday school. You'd fill up the buggy, a two-seater there, and you drove to the church. You couldn't play ball on Sunday and you didn't work, only what you had to do — the chores. It was my dad's and my grandfather's farm before that. I farmed since dad died when he was fifty-nine and I was only thirteen. My brother and I took over the farm. I had to do something because mother was living. I never went to high school because I had to farm.

"I had a tractor and I had a plow and I had a mower and a rake because I couldn't get the hired help otherwise. It was tough enough to farm back then. There was lots of stones. I had to plow twenty or twenty-five acres back then. I quit farming a few years ago."

His well-worn boots.

Jack's favourite pastime.

A portrait of Jack's mother.

Jack King

"This is my father's homestead…"

Ernest St. Louis, Perrault

"I farmed all my life. I have a hundred acres here and I used to cultivate about thirty-five acres. I used to keep ten cows. I stopped farming when I come sixty-five. Ten years I've quit. We started off with sheep and every darn thing but there was no money in that, so at last I just went to cows. I had pure-bred Herefords. This is my father's homestead, he farmed here and cleared this place. It never has changed hands. We started with horses and we'd walk all day. We wouldn't turn too much with a single plow, but it was all right. I thought when I bought a tractor that I'd never get off one, but by God it's damn tiresome too. When you plow till ten o'clock at night you'd be glad to get off. If the ground wasn't so stony it wouldn't jerk you so much."

Ernest still lives on the old homestead.

Ernest St. Louis

The Frasers also have a sawmill.

Betty and Nelson Fraser

"We were three years building the dam."

Nelson Fraser, White Lake

"We use our own power first and then what's left we sell to Ontario Hydro. My dad farmed here, and we have a little land but it's mostly bush. My dad used to always have a few cattle, and we cut some logs. I started the sawmill because the other mill was closing up here, and so I started one just to cut my own stuff, and then I wound up getting a little bigger. We always have hired men down there. We can use the sawmill all year round. I can start it with a diesel, anytime. In the winter everything has to be in real nice shape; in a snowstorm you're plowing snow, and I just don't bother with that. There's a lot of mills that never saw in the winter. You're fighting snow and cold and frost in logs. You get a big round log and get them froze in that far and the rest of it isn't froze and when your saw's going along it won't saw the frozen part. It's a hard job, day after day. I started the sawmill thirty or forty years ago. We mostly cut our own stuff. We do some custom work. Farmers always want a load of logs to build a shed.

"I have a trailer park up there and in a month I could easily run my trailer park with the power I make. I only make thirty-six kilowatts an hour. A kilowatt is like ten, one-hundred-watt bulbs burning for an hour. If I increased my generator to a new model, and my wheel to a new model and everything, I could possibly get more than that. You can't see the water-wheel because the wheel itself is way down at the bottom of a tank, and it's turning there. It's not one of those old clickety wheels like that; it's a large wheel turning on the end of an eighteen-foot shaft, and it's eighteen feet up. We have a big pulley turning here, under the floor, and it goes around, and V-belts run the generator, eight V-belts. We were three years building that dam. We'd work a while, then saw again or cut hay or do something like that and then go back and work at that, when we had time."

Nelson operates a hydro dam on his property.

89

Willard Campbell

"...he just got worse, and he died Friday."

Willard Campbell, White Lake

"I lived around here sixty-eight, pretty near sixty-nine years. My dad died in 1931, and he was fifty-seven. He died of lockjaw. It came from putting out manure; that's what they figure it came from. He didn't know what it was at first, you see; he thought he had a bad cold. It was in late September, and he was at the neighbour's, threshing, and he was running the blower that day. He came home, and he thought he had caught a bad cold, and I can see him yet; I was only ten years old but I can see him, coming walking up from the yard, and he said, 'Oh, I'm sore, I've an awful cold.' That was Thursday and he said, 'I'm going to go out to the doctor tomorrow.' The doctor was coming to White Lake and he had an office on Friday. Well, the next day he said, 'I don't know if I can hitch the horse up or not.' 'Well,' I said, 'I'll hitch it up for you.' And then ma thought, if you're that bad you better stay, and I'll go to neighbour's up here and phone Arnprior and tell him to come down to the house on his way up. And so the doctor came down to the house. Dad told him he had been running the blower and he thought he had the flu. So the doctor gave him sweat tablets and put him to bed. He said, 'You'll get a good sweat with these, and maybe feel better.' Well, the next day he sweated it out, and the doctor came back on Saturday, and dad was feeling a little better, and the doctor gave him some more. By Sunday he wasn't any better, and finally the doctor started to question what dad had been doing

Willard at the kitchen table.

before. Well, he said, he had been putting out manure about three or four weeks before. 'Well, had you any cuts on your hand?' asked the doctor. Yes, he said he had. He'd busted his thumb, hammering a nail in, and of course it was kind of sore, but it was all healed over then, by the time it started to take effect, and there was no sign of it. 'Well,' the doctor said, 'I'm afraid you have lockjaw.' Well, he didn't tell him that, but he told ma that. 'I'll bring another doctor up tonight,' he said. Well, the doctor sent his son to Ottawa that night for he could get no serum. The doctor came up the next day and poured the serum to him, but it was too late. He kind of got a little better for a day or two, and then he just got worse, and he died Friday.

"I was the only one on it, and I never was any professional farmer but I knew how to. I enjoyed farming, but I used to get kind of short of help. I got by anyway."

Willard's ancestors.

Willard's old wood stove.

"You keep your good cattle for breeding..."

Hillais Suddaby, Kemptville

"I never did anything else all my life. I grew up on a farm, and I always farmed. I always had a dairy farm. When we were married we rented a farm for the first three years on a share-share basis, and then, at the end of that time, we bought this farm up there. We bought it in '40. It was near Depression. We kept around eighty Holsteins at the time. I received the Masters Shield in '68. The Holstein Association keep it in line so they figure about a dozen to fifteen are given in Canada each year.

"The breeding of my cattle was the most important thing. The type of cattle and the production has improved tremendously since the time we started. You keep your good cattle for breeding, a lot of people, when the cattle buyer came along and offered them a price for the best cow they had, they sold it, and so they were breeding from the bottom of their herd instead of from the top. You've got to sell the odd one for a good price when you get the opportunity, of course, but, if you don't keep some good breeding stock, you're not going to improve.

"The young people are getting too well educated, and they won't work anymore, a lot of them. They think they're going to sit at a desk and shove a pencil or do a lot of dreaming."

Hillais Suddaby

93

Gordon finally has the time to take it easy.

"I worked it just as if it was my own."

Gordon Craig, Kemptville

"I came here in '36, and I've been here ever since. The woman died in '75, and then Mr. Lewis, he died, it was five years ago last August. Times were hard and I couldn't get a job, and of course, you know, if you have no education, well, it's got to be that you've got a weak mind and a strong back. I worked in the foundries but then they shut up in Merrickville. I had a brother-in-law working here and he hurt his arm, and so I wasn't working at the time, and he asked me if I'd come and work and I said yes. And so I came down and started to work. And they wanted me to stay right on, so I said, you're to go back and ask the other fellow who was here, and he went and asked him, and he didn't want to come back.

"The man that was here, see, he was boss on the county road and the township both, and when I came here I asked him, 'How do you want me to work it?' And he said, 'I want you to work it as though it was your own because you're going to have most of the work to do. I won't be here.' There were lots of days I wouldn't see him at all. We milked fourteen cows by hand. I enjoyed every minute of it because I enjoy animals. When I took over it, I was allowed to sell cattle when the buyers came. After I was here for three years I ran it so we'd have five or six head of cattle to sell every year. I worked it just as if it was my own. I was just so glad to get the chance. I would say it was easier to work the farm in the old days but, at that time, every farm had two and three men. Now you see these men that run the farms today, they don't have time to stop and hardly say, how do you do, to you. That wasn't the way with us when we farmed.

"I couldn't say enough good about the people here, they were just swell. The nicest place I ever got into."

Gordon Craig

Leo and Mary O'Neill

"We didn't go on a honeymoon."

Leo and Mary O'Neill, Oxford Mills

"My father started farming right over here on this hill. I was born over there and lived a year there and then I came over here and lived here till I was eighteen and then I went back there and lived there till I was married and then we came back here. I worked out a lot of the time. I worked at the cheese business at Oxford Station, in storage. They picked up the cheese from the factories and they had a grading station there. It's all gone by the way now. I was foreman out there at that cheese plant for some twenty years. She looked after the farm when I was working.

"We milked in the morning, and we had pigs and I'd feed the pigs. We were up at five o'clock every morning to do the chores. Women always had to get out and help milk, especially when you were milking by hand, and you'd wash up the milking equipment. During haying and that, women worked. They drove horses and they drove the rake and that kind of work. That was before tractors and balers."

"We were married in Kemptville at Holy Cross Church going on forty-seven years this June. We didn't go on a honeymoon. We got up the next morning and milked. We lived over there for the first few weeks and then we came over here. This place had to be all fixed up. This never was intended to be used again. Nobody had lived here since he was eighteen."

George Consitt

"You don't know what you're worth till you sell out."

George Consitt, Perth

"There's not a lot of money in farming compared to other jobs where they get a hundred dollars a day for an eight-hour day. You make it all right but then it all goes back into the farm. You don't know what you're worth till you sell out. There's a lot of jobs you do out on a farm that you really do for the satisfaction of it. You know there's not much money. There's nothing worse than picking stone and you go out to a big field and you start picking stone and it's hard to see where the return will come other than the fact that the stones are not going to get into the machinery and break the machinery. Or if you clear brush, you don't see any great increase in your cheque that you get from the dairy or whatever. It's a way of life. But I'm afraid that as the farms get bigger, it gets to be a business, not a way of life. Maybe I'm wrong but for me it was seeing what I could do with the farm.

"I raised chickens for a while and I used to peddle them around town. It was mixed farming back then. You had eggs and you had pigs and you had cows. I think one of the biggest changes on the farm is when electricity came; that was a big thing. It was great to have lights out in the barn. Then we got the water for the cows in the barn and I think it was quite a change. When you'd put cows out and maybe it'd be twenty-five below and you used to have to go clean to the creek back there and chop a hole in the ice and let them get a drink."

The Donohues' sons Mike and Patrick have now taken over the farm.

*Ozzie and Velma
Donohue*

"...my boys are taking over here."

Ozzie Donohue, Eganville

"We're here thirty-seven years maybe. My wife, she was born here. I remember when we bought the place there was an old gentleman up here and he said, 'I heard you bought the farm.' And I said, 'Yes.' 'Well,' he said, 'I'm going to give you a piece of advice.' He said, 'There will be days when you'll feel like throwing up your hands and saying the heck with it. And,' he said, 'you'll go to bed that night and have a sleep, and you'll get up the next morning and everything will look a little different. That's the only way to look at it, because,' he said, 'if you think you're going to go to bed at night and get up in the morning and be happy, I'll tell you, you're crazy.'

"I'm not farming now; my boys are taking over here. All I do is look after a few hens here and keep myself in eggs. They have cows and calves now."

"I loved the farm and I loved my cows."

Bill and Ada McRoberts, Winchester

"I was born in Glasgow, Scotland, and my dad was killed in the First World War and mother was left with five kids. When we came here at first we lived right in Mountain. I was twelve years old in January and I left home in Febuary and old Mr. Boyd, Leroy Boyd, had a farm just east of Hallville church and I went to work there at twelve years old. I was there for two years. I then went to work for the Van Allen people, and I was there for almost twelve years and we were married there and our oldest daughter was born there. Then we bought this farm here north of town and farmed there for thirty years.

"I fell off the barn years ago. We had a barn down the field and the roof had been let go and the shingles were gone. In those times, during the War, steel roofing was hard to get but I got a chance to get the stuff for the roof from this guy. We had the crop in and I said, 'Well I guess I better go down and get the shingles off the roof so it will be ready when the steel comes.' I went down in the morning and I got up on the roof and had the old shovel and I was shoveling the shingles off. I came up for dinner and the truck came in with the steel and the driver said that the guy I bought the steel from would be down next day to help me put it on. So after dinner I said, 'I better go down and get the roof ripped off.' And so I went down in the middle of the afternoon and I guess I was hurrying too much and I guess I should've taken another board up for a toe-hold and anyway I slipped and I went off and I hurt my back. There was a well at the corner of the barn and I went down and had a drink of water and went back up and finished the roof. Then this Leroy Boyd used to come back to the farm for eggs and berries and he came back this day, it was in October and it was a miserable, wet day, and my back was awful bad that day and he said, 'Why don't you get a job and get away from some of this hard work?' 'Well,' I said, 'What will I do at my age and no education? Who would want me?' 'Did you ever think of selling cars?' he asked. And I said, 'Well no, that's the last job in the world I want.' He said, 'You think about it.' So I thought about it. That was in October and so the first week of February Boyd pulled up and he said, 'Come on out this afternoon Scot'; they never called me anything else but Scot. I went out and he and his two sons got me in the office and he wanted to know if I had thought anything about it and I said I thought about it all right. The more I thought about it the less it appealed to me. To start with, I knew nothing about cars and less about salesmanship. He said, 'I don't agree with you Scot, you're well-known and well-thought-of and I think you can go out and talk to farmers in their own language.' So anyway I started to sell cars and I was on my twentieth year when I quit. If I could've farmed I would of definitely stayed on the farm. I loved the farm and I loved my cows.

"Her people were on a farm up about two miles from where I worked at Van Allen's and we went to the Van Camp church and she chased me till I caught her. Fifty-nine years ago on the third of June. We didn't have a big wedding."

" I was born right there at Winchester Station. There was a school teacher that boarded at Van Allen's and taught in the little school just below the house and we thought quite a lot of her. She married a guy from Hallville who was a minister and he had his first church at Rideau Ferry. We thought a lot of both of them and we asked them if they would marry us. So the Van Allens took us up there. We bought the farm four years later but before that we lived with the Van Allens. We didn't have the money to start out and buy a farm."

Ada and Bill McRoberts

Photos of Ada and Bill.

"...you'd get a cent a pound for them."

Art Curry, Kemptville

"I went to Detroit and worked there for a year and then I came back, just for a holiday, and my father, who was still selling cows, asked me if I'd stay and work with him. I was the oldest son and I was the only one that drove the car at that time so, in about 1924, I started working with him driving around and buying cows and selling them. Then I got married in about 1930. Before I got married I had a good-size bush and I had cut a bunch of these pine trees and got a lot of lumber and I figured to build a house sometime. And so I took it down to McMaster's Mill and got it planed up and I hired Howard Perkins as the carpenter at four dollars a day and his board: dinner and supper.

"I shipped milk when I first started farming and I separated the milk and took the milk to the creamery in Kemptville. Then I took it to the cheese factory down below Kemptville because they were paying about five cents a hundred pounds more. At the creamery I'd figure on getting forty-five cents a hundred for my milk by separating it, and I got fifty-five cents a hundred by taking it to the cheese factory. Then I quit the cheese factory and I shipped to Libby's for quite a while, out of Brockville. And then they'd pay you so much to grow cucumbers and I started putting in acres of cucumbers. They'd pick them up the same time they'd pick the milk up.

"I enjoyed farming, you were your own boss. I mind one time when I was at home there and I was looking at the paper seeing if there was any farms for sale and I said to mother, 'I think I'd like to be a farmer.' 'Well,' she said, 'if you can stand lots of worry go ahead.' In the old days I've sold cows for twenty-five dollars a cow. Back in the '30s they weren't worth nothing. I used to go out through the country and buy canner cows for five or six dollars a cow and you'd get a cent a pound for them. You'd bring them home and take them out to the station there and sell them for a cent a pound. I've seen where they had a big fifteen-hundred-pound bull there one time and got a cent a pound, fifteen dollars. That was back in the Depression you know.

"Nobody wants to work on a farm anymore and you can't blame them when you think. When I was shipping the milk, you had to have it back there at eight o'clock in the morning which means you had to get up at a quarter to five every morning."

Art Curry

"They're farming different now."

Ralph and Nobel Eady, Castleford

"When you go to buy something they tell you what to pay, and when you go to sell something they tell you what they're going to give you. So you have no figuring at all to do. I farm just about two miles from here. I bought the place in 1953. I work out and sublet the farm now. They're farming different now. They always used to have a few cows around and have the cream cheque coming, but now a lot of guys have no cattle at all and the other guy has a whole bunch. In '39 it started to pick up when the war started and then in '40 I worked for the railroad for a couple of years for thirty-five cents an hour, and that was good. It was good money, ten dollars a month.

"I heard this story when they were interviewing people. They interviewed this young fellow about twenty, and asked him what would you do if you got a million dollars? Well, the young fellow said he'd get himself a nice little cottage and a nice convertible and a girlfriend and he'd really sport around and have a good time. So they asked this other fellow, a school teacher, and he had big ideas and he thought he'd get some kind of boat that he could have dances on and that and he'd live a life like that. And then they asked this old farmer what he'd do if he got a million dollars. 'Well,' he says, 'I'd buy a wee bit more land and get some better machinery and I'd farm away while the money lasted.'"

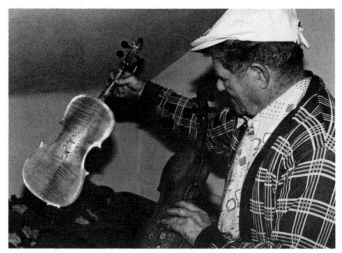

Ralph shows his collection of fiddles.

Around the kitchen table.

Ralph and Noble Eady

Eva and Barclay Dick

"You have to keep it true to variety."

Barclay Dick, Douglas

"We were burned out in the Scotch Bush in '31, and we had to move some place, so we moved out here, and we bought this place over there. When we farmed here first, we sent to the cheese factory for a number of years. We then changed our methods a bit, and we went to seed grain and beef cattle. As far as I was concerned I was always interested in a good way of farming. My father wasn't interested in clay land and that's why, when we moved from the Scotch Bush, he moved back a few years after and he put up a building out there.

"What's here is clay. We grow barley, wheat, oats, and we've kept up over the times with the new varieties. We started in then, getting the breeder seed from the Department of Agriculture. We generally watch for new varieties coming in to being and they don't always prove out great, either. You have to be in it to do it. I did get very good co-operation from the Canadian Seed Growers and also from Kemptville. The whole thing is to keep it true. You have to keep it true to variety. You have a lot of work to do a good job, and of course, in the later years, I don't think people are doing a good job. I can remember we got seed from Winnipeg, and I had it shipped down here, and I got a couple of stocks of wheat in it, and so it wasn't perfect. Any of it is ninety-nine-per-cent pure; you just can't say it is a hundred per cent. When you get into seed you have to be a little better than the next guy. My idea through the time was to satisfy the customer, and then they'll come back. I say now, if the average farmer farms long enough, the way things are, he'll likely go broke."

One of Barclay's many awards.

"We used to eat four meals a day."

Martin Hass, Shamrock

"I worked on straightening the road out to Mount St. Patrick for eighty-eight cents a day. I was born down on the Eleventh Concession, down here about two and a half miles. My dad bought the farm before he was married, and he was too young to sign it so my dad gave my grandfather the money, and then when he came of age my grandfather signed it back to him for a dollar.

"Most of the year dad cut wood and drew it to Renfrew, fourteen miles, up and down the roads. He used to be drawing it in the winter-time, and I often heard him saying that one time he run two trips in one day. He had two teams of horses, eh, and he went down hill about two miles below Shamrock, and he met Doctor Mann with the cutter. Doctor Mann was heading to Griffith to tend someone who was sick. My dad went down with the load, and he got back in late afternoon and had lunch and put on another load of wood. He took the other team of horses and took it down. So at about half past seven at night, dad was coming up here, and Doctor Mann was just coming back from Griffith, and he says to dad, 'I thought I was the hardest-working man in the country, but I think you've got me beat.'

"We used to eat four meals a day. We'd get up about half past five and if the horses were in the stables, we'd feed them, and if the horses were out in the pasture where there was lots of good grass, we'd leave them out, and then you'd go out to the pasture and bring the horses in and maybe give them a feed of oats and have them all ready for seven o'clock. And then we'd come in about half past ten maybe for dinner, and then about three or three-thirty we used to call it tea, and then we'd work till dark. That was a long day especially around haying time. If it looked like rain, we worked half the night to get that hay coiled so it wouldn't get spoiled.

"There was no trucking cattle in those days, eh. In the fall of the year they'd come down in droves and maybe a hundred or more head in one drove. One thing this country is lacking now is the sheep business. I can remember sitting in that school, and there was a field across there about an acre size, and there was about three or four hundred sheep. They'd gather them from Griffith and Mount St. Patrick and everybody that sold their sheep, and they'd all join in the bunch, eh, and there was no way of moving them but in the drove, and they'd drive them right up through Renfrew into the pens there, and then ship them in the cars. They'd bring the droves down the highway from Mount St. Patrick, and there wasn't hardly a car on the road them days. Maybe there was three cars in Mount St. Patrick, and maybe they'd only go out once or twice a week."

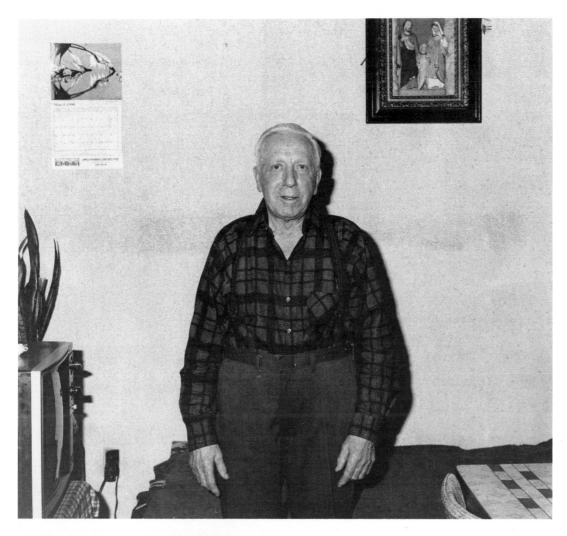

Martin Hass

Martin's home in Shamrock.

Hattie and Eric Timm

"You're your own boss..."

Eric Timm, Eganville

"I was born on the farm and when my father passed away, well I was twenty when I took it over. I farmed till 1931 and then I went off the farm and I worked out as a labourer in a sawmill. I stopped farming because of my health. For a couple of years I didn't work at all. I worked in a sawmill for thirty-four years. I would rather have farmed. You're your own boss, and I liked working in the bush and in the fields and out in the open air. It was no easy job in the sawmill. Now it's okay, they all have automatic levers and rollers. You don't lift a pound. But out there you bring them in sixteen feet long, maple and oak, and then you square them down. And I tell you they're coming one after another. You lift one seven-by-nine oak green lumber, you're lifting I'm telling you. Heavy work. I used to walk a good five miles to the mill one way and then walk back, and that's ten miles a day I walked, every day, winter and summer. I'd leave at six in the morning and be home at six at night. I was sixty-eight when I quit there.

"When I was on the farm it was all horses, there was no tractors, there was no nothing. I liked that, I liked the horses, especially plowing. I loved plowing. You could get every furrow that wide. I plowed out at the neighbours when I lived out there and I used to average two acres a day. I'd use all kinds of horses. At one place across there I had a team of westerns, they had white feet and white faces and they were good, they were quick.

"I farmed back through the Depression, back in '29, '30, '31. They were bad. A pound of butter, fifteen cents, a dozen of eggs, six cents. You couldn't make a dollar. I had year-old cattle and I sold them for six dollars a piece and I sold the two-year-olds for twelve dollars. I had a three-hundred-acre farm. I used to cut a lot of wood, too. I used to cut maybe a hundred and fifty cords in the winter, all two-foot wood. By golly I drew it all here to Eganville for two dollars a cord."

"...it just came out of the ground in truck loads."

Wilkie Seabrook, Stittsville

"I had a difficult time when I started to farm. That was back in '33. I rented a farm for the first year, from my aunt, and things didn't turn out very good. A fellow was helping us bale the hay so I could move it, and he just mentioned to my father that he would sell his place if he got anything at all for it. It was only fifty acres, and that was really more then I could afford to buy, but we did buy and started from there. I raised a lot of chickens at first, and then eventually I got into the livestock business. Farming is much easier today; there's more equipment available, and at that time there was a lot of physical work.

"I got out of farming, I farmed for ten years for nothing; I didn't make any money so I thought I'd try something else. So I bought a little feed business in Stittsville. I had a farm sale and sold everything I had, which wasn't a lot. But this feed business, I was a little disappointed; I could see this wasn't for me because you never had any time for yourself at noon; there was always somebody around looking for something, right when you're trying to have your lunch-hour. It was a pretty small, little business, only one man and myself. I tried it for five months, and then I got a chance to sell it, and I was happy to do that. Even at that time there was a change coming: fewer dealers and bigger dealers.

"So, when I sold the feed business, I decided I really did want to farm, and so I got the chance to buy a farm from my uncle. I decided that I should try and build it up a bit, so I bought some fertilizer and put it on, and the results were just unbelievable. I was growing grain and hay, and it just came out of the ground in truck loads. Fertilizer wasn't used much back then; it was all new around here. We were always using manure, but some of these farms were too far away to put manure on them. That was in 1945. In the fall of '47, there was a farm over near Richmond for sale. They tried to sell it through public auction. I wasn't at the sale the day it came up, and I kind of forgot about it. Anyhow, they sold a little bit of chattels, but the farm was still for sale. So a few days later I was going over to Richmond on the Shea Road, and this fellow stopped me and said to me, 'Have you changed your mind?' And I said, 'No, you must have the wrong guy.' Anyway we talked a little while and he said, 'You should buy this place.' There was no fences, and the roofs were all off the buildings, and everything was in pretty bad shape — the house wasn't too bad. He kind of coaxed me to make him an offer, and I did. He said, 'You'll likely hear from me in a few days.' And I did. I bought a farm. Just like that. The trouble with farming today is the investment is too great for the income. High interest rates now are just ruining the farmer."

Wilkie Seabrook

Archie Hawthorne.

"I miss the horses..."

Archie Hawthorne, Ferguson Falls

"I was raised up about three and a half miles up the old highway to Beachburg. Then I farmed just at the house coming into the Falls and our land went back along the Cobden Road. That's where I put in forty-five years. There was six of us in the family and we all had to get out on farms of our own when we got married. We all farmed and we never worked out, either, when we were at home. We had enough land to keep us all working, all the boys. You plowed with a one-furrow plow with the horses. We had quite a bit of land and we kept a lot of stock and at that time it was done by hand, there was no big machines. I was ten or twelve when we got the

first hay loader. It didn't take much money back then.

"I miss the horses but the time had come when I couldn't do anything with them. I like Clydes. Up at home we had a stable for thirty-six and if we had any more some of the cows or the bull or somebody had to stay out to make room for the horses. We raised an awful lot of horses. We bought them and sold them and at that time the farmers counted on horses and every spring they'd be looking for horses to put the crop in. I started first with the sulky plow, I wasn't old enough for to handle a walking plow. The first pure-bred stallion I mind was bought in 1913. The reason I remember about the stallion was because the *Titanic* went down in 1912 and there was a couple who went over to Scotland from Ottawa and they bought a stallion over there and they were coming back on the *Titanic* and they went down. This horse we bought was brought into Ottawa to the fair and they put him into a box stall there and we were to get him after the fair was over. And there was this horse that came from Scotland and he had a bigger name and the owners were bigger and so they got them to take our horse out of this stall and they put this other horse from Scotland in the box stall right over the big boiler. But before the fair was over, the boiler exploded and the horse went through the roof. That's the reason I remember all that. It saved our horse. The people that bought him went down with the *Titanic* and the horse was blown up too. That was at the Ottawa Winter Fair and it was in January at that time."

Archie donates a trophy to the Cobden Fair each year.

"If I were a young man, I'd still be farming."

A lifetime of farming hasn't been enough for Bert Spratt. The ninety-year-old sits in his home on the outskirts of Richmond, speaking wistfully of the work and the long hours, the cows and the corn, the independence and the traditional farm life he knows so well.

"Oh, I enjoyed farming," he says. "I enjoyed everything: the different jobs, experimenting and watching stuff grow, improving from one year to another, you know."

"I have no regrets. I'd do it all the same," he says, slamming his hands on the arms of his chair for emphasis.

Bert retired in 1965 after a half-century of farming. His present home sits on a corner of what was once part of his one-hundred-and-thirty-five-acre spread. He sold eighty-six acres to the government for a sewage lagoon in 1964: "Then there wasn't enough left to farm," Bert says. A greenhouse business sits on another corner now. The rest is growing up in weeds and saplings, but at one time it was one of the best farms in the area.

Bert was born into the farming life in 1900. His parents owned a five-hundred-and-fifty-acre farm at the junction of Walkley and Heron Roads in Ottawa. His grandfather cleared the land around 1880, and the last acres were sold to the National Capital Commission in 1973.

"Holy jumpin' we had a lot of buildings there and one hundred and seventy-five dairy cattle," says Bert. "Now you go down there and you wouldn't know where it was. All I recognize is the railroad tracks."

Bert was the sixth-born of thirteen children, four boys and nine girls. By the time he was ten years old, Bert was out with the walking plow, and when he completed grade eight he became a full-time farmer. "Lots never went even half way through school. I know my figures though. I would take some stuff to a sale and I could figure it out in my head faster than a guy can on paper," he says. "And I'm experienced in farming. That's something you can't buy or learn in school. It takes years of doing it."

His experience includes a year's work on a thirty-six-hundred-acre farm in Bradwell, Saskatchewan, in 1928. "That was the best experience a man ever got. I learned all about their type of farming," says Bert. It was truly farming on a grand scale; the farm had forty-two horses and seven mules. In an old photograph, piles of straw look like miniature mountains along the prairie skyline.

Bert spent the winter of 1929 and 1930 working in a Detroit car factory. "I wasn't sure if I wanted to farm or not when I saw the other lads. At six o'clock they'd come home and they'd be off till the next morning and they had holidays and here I had to go to work." Seven months in Detroit convinced him. "As soon as the grass started getting green you couldn't hold me in," he says. "I think farming's the best job."

His father, Tom Spratt died shortly after Bert got home; his older brother got the farm and Bert got some money which he used to buy his Richmond farm. It was 1930 and "everybody was broke." "Those were hard times. You had to have some

Bert Spratt

One of Bert's many awards.

experience or you'd never have got it started. My father taught me well. I knew everything."

Bert bought the farm on the first of November and plowed thirty-five acres before the land froze. "I'd take my lunch and a nosebag for the horse and I'd start at five in the morning and I wouldn't come back till nine at night. I just stayed right out there to get it plowed. They wouldn't do that now. If you missed a meal nowadays it would be an awful thing. Those were the days," he says.

He borrowed money to buy livestock and fix his house, which the previous owners had used as a stable for eighteen cows. He milked his Holsteins by hand, and got through that first winter. Bert pauses to look at his right hand which is large enough to pick up a basketball. "I wear a size-twelve ring," he says. "That's from all those years of milking."

He milked his Holsteins by hand for the first two years before he bought a milking machine. "We used to get eight cents a hundred (pounds) for our milk. No wonder people paid only ten cents a quart at the store."

Despite the hard work, Bert always had enough energy for a party. "I love a party and I've had my share of them," he says. "We'd drive twenty-five or thirty miles with horses to a dance. We'd leave for the party early in the evening and we'd stay late. We'd dance till three in the morning. So long as we got home for the milking."

He met his first wife, a Kemptville government worker named Beatrice Wilson, during a sleigh

A view of Bert's old farm.

ride in January 1931. They were married by April. "I liked the farm and she did the housework and looked after the chickens," says Bert.

The couple had no children but they had a mixed farm with a bit of everything else including dairy and beef cattle, pigs, horses and chickens. Before he went into dairy in 1942, he raised two hundred pigs a year.

"I kept buying the little ones from Martin Kennedy and selling him the big ones. They'd fight for the first while. Oh yeah, they were vicious. You had to introduce them to each other. You'd put them in the pen for a while and then take them out. Then you'd take some manure from the new pig and scatter it over the pigs and change the smell," says Bert. "I was glad to get rid of the pigs in one way but they were money makers; mortgage lifters we called them."

By 1942, Bert had forty Holsteins and fifty beef cattle "all makes." Then for three years the banks of the Jock River flooded his barnyard. "The first time it just started to rain one night at about four o'clock and the next morning it was waist-high in my stable. I had to move the cows at night upstairs in the barn. We didn't take the hens out and in the morning they were in the water, floating on the straw; you could see their heads.

We had to fish them out and we never lost a hen."

In addition to livestock, Bert tended a wide variety of crops. He says that he loved to watch things growing. "I tried everything: soya beans, green peas, barley, oats, corn. Darn right, whatever paid. I sold green peas for green pea soup, for ten years, to Nat Lindsay. He and Mack Anderson, the head of the North Star grist mill in Carp, were partners. They were just wonderful to deal with."

In 1932 he decided to rent land around him, and by 1942 he was renting nearly four hundred acres a year. "I didn't need to buy feed or fertilizer. It kept us busy, you were never out of a job."

One of his favourite things in the early days was working with the neighbours at "thrashing" time. "We had seventeen farms on our circuit. They'd follow the thrashing mill right along and the women did the cooking for us. Some farms would be bigger than the others; the odd guy would just have a few acres, but he'd stay right with the gang. We were given a banquet every time we had a meal. No wonder they stayed! I've seen three or four jugs of milk on a table, roast beef, vegetables, potatoes, gravy, two or three kinds of pies, great big dishes of applesauce. It was a nice sociable time. Now there are no neighbours at all. I don't know if they're too busy or just don't care."

The threshing circuit ended when farmers started to buy machines. Bert bought the area's first tractor in 1936 for six hundred dollars, and he bought the first combine in 1948, an International, for seventeen hundred dollars. "I could see where the new machines would help. I go to those antique machinery shows and ninety-five per cent of the stuff there I've used before. I know how to fix half of it too."

Usually Bert had three hired men, sometimes five, who Bert says were like family to him. "Oh, they were really good lads." Some of the men went on to very good careers; one became the manager of the Niagara Falls park, another boy from England, later became the president of Shell Oil. "You learn a lot by farming. It gives you business sense, no doubt about it," says Bert. After the Second World War, though, it was harder to get hired men so Bert had to buy bigger machinery.

Despite his extensive farming operation, Bert took time to sit on the Richmond Fair Board for thirty-eight years, including six years as president. "I didn't show at the fair, I was more interested in getting the fair to pay. I can do the figuring. That's the whole darn thing — deciding what you want and then getting it. You have to know the value of things."

When he first started farming, he promised himself he'd stop milking when he turned sixty. True to his resolve, he called in the auctioneer after his sixtieth birthday, but he kept beef cattle a few more years. "I liked farming but it was getting where everything was too expensive. And every time you turn around someone else had their hand in it."

Beatrice Spratt died in 1977 and a few years later Bert married Ann Gault, ten years his junior and a friend of his late wife's sister. Over the years, the couple has kept busy curling, bowling, dancing, playing bridge and travelling. Now Bert's health is failing and today he sits in his armchair gazing at the neighbour's soya bean crop across the road.

"If I were a young man, I'd still be farming. I love the farm," he says. "I'd just love to be out there on the machines, with the dust blowing."

Chapter Three

I Wouldn't
Do Anything
Else.

"I couldn't sit here and farm and not do something..."

Twenty-one years ago Raye-Anne Briscoe was a greenhorn farmer. She thought all grain was yellow and didn't know the difference between a heifer and a steer. Today, Raye-Anne not only runs a successful dairy farm in partnership with her husband John, she's also a tireless lobbyist in Ottawa for the National Farmers' Union.

As the organization's executive assistant, she presents the farmer's case to high-powered bureaucrats and leading politicians. Basically, Raye-Anne thinks that farmers have the right to make a decent living: "Farmers cannot live with markets where it's a case of, 'What are you going to give me for my product?' and their expenses are, 'What do I have to pay?' There's no control. It's unworkable in any industry," she says.

She knows farming: the statistics, the heart-breaking failures, the prices, the problems and the rewards. She credits the Farmers' Union with providing the information she needs. Informing farmers, she says, is still the Union's most important function.

Raye-Anne was born and raised in Renfrew where her father owned Renfrew Textiles. When Raye-Anne and John married in 1962, he was a Pembroke truck driver and she was an elementary school teacher. Seven years later they decided to return to John's father's dairy farm in Admaston Township. Today, they have two hundred and twenty acres of prime agricultural land off the Bonnechere River, in what's known as the Brulis, where they breed and milk seventy Holsteins.

John joined the National Farmers' Union in 1970, and Raye-Anne became active in 1973. "I only had a very limited amount of time to spend with any farm organization because I was working full-time off the farm. With the NFU I could see good, positive results. I was included, even as a person from town. My ideas were listened to. The NFU is a grass-roots movement," says Raye-Anne.

The National Farmers' Union, based in Saskatoon, Saskatchewan, was founded in 1969, and has chapters in nine of the ten provinces; Quebec has its own farm organization. Today the Farmers' Union has twenty-five thousand farm-family members - a total of at least fifty thousand farmers. In the Ottawa Valley about five hundred families are members. The union is funded solely through membership fees. For $130 a year, a family receives a monthly newsletter, a newspaper every six weeks, information and representation.

"Through the NFU you really get a perspective of national agriculture. You understand that the grain industry is the basis of all agriculture's successes and failures. You understand how the grain industry works in this country. Policy is established based not on the problems of one area but on the national situation. This understanding of the whole industry helps to broaden a farmer's perspective and that helps him or her to be a better farmer. I know it has helped me," says Raye-Anne.

She also likes the fact that both men and women are encouraged to get involved in the NFU. "Women and men are farmers. I'm not a farmer's wife, or a farm person. I'm a farmer."

As Raye-Anne learned more about farming and the National Farmers' Union, she saw her opportunity to contribute. She began by serving on various local committees and in 1978 was elected President of local 350, covering the area from Renfrew to Cobden. Then, from 1985 to 1988, she served as the Ontario co-ordinator, the union's highest provincial office. Raye-Anne is concerned about the future of farming, not only in the Ottawa Valley but across Canada.

According to Raye-Anne, the farmers' biggest problem is the low prices they receive for their products. "Commodity prices must be based on the cost of production, including labour and interest rates. The food-processing industry is making more money than ever; it's the farmer who isn't receiving a fair price," says Raye-Anne.

The Milk Marketing Board and Feather Marketing Board have helped to stabilize those commodity prices so that the farmer can earn a living. The farmer gets forty-five cents for a litre of milk, seventy-five cents for a pound of butter, sixty cents for a dozen eggs.

"The price for your turkey last Christmas was the same as the Christmas before. That's under a regulated system, but farmers can make a living," says Raye-Anne.

Farmers with products which don't have a marketing board are having problems, she says. Hog producers get about sixty cents a pound, dressed, and it costs them about a dollar a pound to raise the animal. Beef farmers get seventy to seventy-five cents a pound on the hoof, about the same as the cost of production. Grain growers receive seven cents for each loaf of bread.

"It's terrible the gouging that goes on; the consumer receives absolutely no benefit from these low farm prices, and the farmer suffers,"

says Raye-Anne. The NFU wants marketing boards for all farm products, to guarantee farmers a price. "Supply management has terrible connotations, but it's the same theory used in any industry. Markets are researched, costs are determined and a price is set. Each farmer controls their production. It has a dirty name but it's just good business."

She concedes that farmers are often their own worst enemies. "Farmers are jittery and they aren't prone to change. There was a big struggle, and it took a lot of courage by elected people to put milk marketing in place, because they didn't necessarily have the broad support of the farmers and there was a lot of opposition from consumers," says Raye-Anne. "Farmers are split. Maybe some day we will unite."

"But the fact of the matter is that right now there's no profit for many farmers." Raye-Anne gazes out her picture window onto their green front field. "Just down the road, Harold Lynch had over four hundred acres with a full cow-calf feedlot operation and there isn't a cow on his land now, hasn't been any for three years."

"We're the only country in the world that has no import controls on beef. There are no rules and regulations on the industry so prices continue to drop to a point where a living can't be made. Beef farmers have to have jobs outside the farm which means they automatically cut down on their herd size."

Two-thirds of all Canadian farmers' income is now earned off the farm. "It's very difficult to find any farm where there isn't some kind of outside income," says Raye-Anne. "The beef industry is limping along as a hobby. In another generation it will be gone. A forty-year-old guy is going to hold

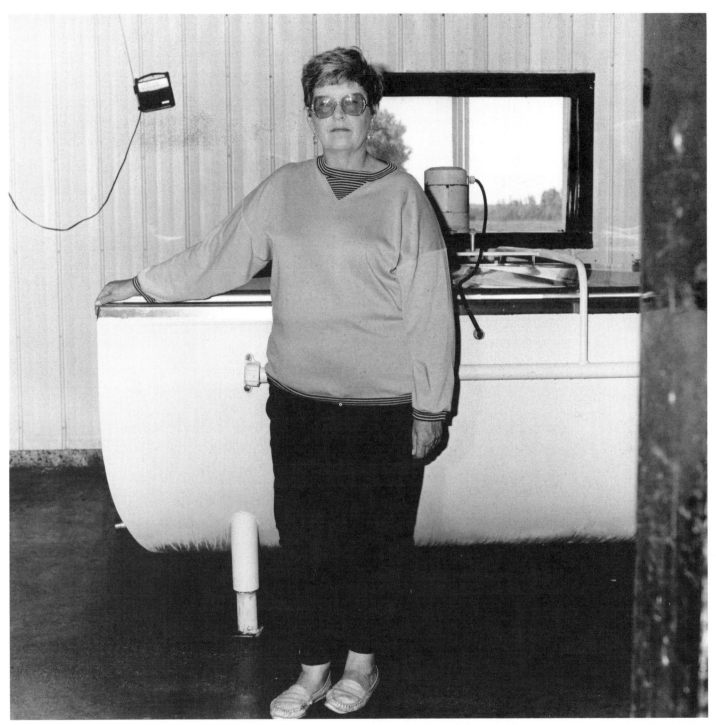

Raye-Anne Briscoe

another job but his son or daughter isn't. Who needs it?"

A common misconception is that family farms are handed down from generation to generation without any cost. "You can't give the farm to your children because if you haven't made a living then your retirement plan is your farm," says Raye-Anne. "The kids have to borrow the money all over again. We're refinancing these farms every generation and that's a heavy burden."

Raye-Anne spends a lot of time talking to consumers, getting their support for farmers.

"The farming population in Canada now accounts for less than three per cent of the total population so it's important, it's essential, that we inform Canadians about agriculture. We can't save ourselves; it doesn't matter how a farmer votes any more because the numbers aren't there," says Raye-Anne.

That's why she's a strong proponent of coalitions in her present job as the first and only national farming-organization lobbyist in Canada, a paid position she has held since January 1989.

The National Farmers' Union first became involved in coalitions when Raye-Anne sat on Pro-Canada Network which opposed the Canada-U.S. Free Trade Agreement. "A coalition really broadens our base. You have someone from ACTRA (Alliance of Canadian Cinema, Television and Radio Artists) saying we need grain farmers in this country, and I'm saying we have to protect our Canadian authors. I think that's the future of the Canadian justice movement," says Raye-Anne.

A familiar sign on many farms.

Raye-Anne has been an active member of the NFU since 1973.

As a lobbyist, she also sits in on federal agriculture committee meetings. She has presented the farmers' case to numerous Ministers of Parliament, to the Newfoundland Minister of Agriculture, to embassies and at conferences. Her NFU contract says that she's to work two days a week in Ottawa and half-time at home but it's more than a full-time job.

"I'm devoted. I understand agriculture and that has given me control. I couldn't sit here and farm and not do something about it. I couldn't let the whole thing fall down around everybody's ears."

Allan's dog follows him everywhere.

Ruth and Allan Foster

"We've cut back an awful lot now..."

Allan Foster, North Gower

"I came over here in 1959 and bought this old farm and some colts. When we were kids at home that's all we used on the farm. We farmed with horses and my dad used to raise two or three foals every year and we'd break colts. We've cut back an awful lot now, after thirty years of farming and then both of us were born on the farm too. It's a good life but you have to like it or you wouldn't be doing it. I remember when we lived back where the golf course is; all the farmers cut wood by the acre lots. There'd be maybe a dozen teams, when we were walking home from school, coming out there with big loads of wood and drawing it all down to Merivale Road, to Woodroffe Avenue and to the farms. My dad was a good farmer. We milked cows and we used to have to buy a lot of hay and draw a lot of feed in.

"There was a lot of boys, when we were first married, that came up from Nova Scotia and Newfoundland looking for jobs. One time we had about four out of a family. The younger ones would come up and they'd go and they'd send up some more. Their family would keep writing to us, asking if we'd take another. I remember one time we went into the train station and this young kid, who had never left home in his life, had come all the way from Belle Isle. He was here for quite a while. They were real good kids. Once they got a few dollars the main thing was they had to get to Toronto."

Bill used this old threshing-machine for many years.

Bill Hutchins and his wife Elizabeth.

"I saw us threshing on the fourth of December."

Bill Hutchins, Oxford Mills

"My father started out threshing with a steam-engine for his father, at fourteen years old. His father died when he was only about twenty-three. My father kept on threshing, and he threshed right from Donny Ralph's right straight through to the other side of Bishops, and up that way and down this way. He'd leave in August for stook threshing, and he wouldn't be home till November. He'd be home at nights but, if he was way back there, he may not come home at night. He could do his own repairs on the mill, a lot of it. But he did not work on Sunday. He didn't believe in work on Sunday, and I think he was farther ahead.

"I just threshed for a couple of years, and then the combine came in. I was on the farm here, I done the farming. He wasn't a farmer. That's funny. My father wasn't really a farmer; he didn't have enough time. He done carpentry work, he done custom threshing, he done custom work out in the field with the tractor in the spring of the year, and in the winter-time he had his little workshop over in there, and he could turn out neck yokes or if somebody broke the tongue out of their sleigh or something like that. He worked in there. That's how we made our bread and butter.

"A combine is a time-saver, but you get far better grain with a threshing-machine. It was cut, stooked and it sort of dried in the stook. Now you can combine it, you think it's dry, but if there's a little bit of green in it, you got to put a drier in and watch it don't heat the bin. But you never had that bother with threshing with the threshing-machine.

"That was always one thing with us here, we always had to do our's last. I saw us threshing on the fourth of December. We got up one morning, and there was snow on the ground, and dad said, 'I guess we better thresh today.' We went at it, and it never bothered him, and it was pretty nippy that day. But I'm telling you, the grain just came out of there like shot, just as dry and hard. We didn't do that every year of course, but I remember the one year."

Heavy horses are still kept on the Hutchins' farm.

"We have a little bit of everything."

Bill Stewart, Pakenham

"I've been here thirty-three years. I was working for a farmer, and I worked down there from 1950 till 1956, and I moved up here in the spring. When I came up here I had twenty-nine head of cattle gathered up, and I brought the team of horses they had down there with me, he didn't like horses anyway, and he wasn't going to use them. This place was here, and it belonged to my wife's father so I rented it for six years, and I bought it in 1962. We have beef and dairy and a little bit of everything. The only thing we don't have right now is any pigs, but we're going to get some before too long. My son works with me, and he'll eventually take over the farm.

"We go to the Pakenham dances and I haven't missed one since they started. Those kinds of dances have been the tradition for years. At one time it was just about gone. We have six squares there, every dance."

Bill with one of his ponies.

Bill Stewart

George Pirie

"We have no choice now."

George Pirie, Bristol

"We own three hundred acres and we have a hundred and fifty acres rented. Dad purchased this farm in 1927. He was born and raised in Clarendon, and he was in his mid-twenties when he bought this farm. We're a dairy farm, pure-bred Holsteins. Over the years we've tried to specialize in the export market for any surplus livestock. We milk fifty cows and we have in total, counting young stock, around a hundred and twenty-five. We could milk seventy, we have seventy-one comfort stalls here in the barn. But

we have to feed and there's the quota and the prices — we try and keep it as a family farm. There have been periodic times that we have a man for a few months but we find now we can hire students in the summer.

"We have our own machines for hay and we have our own machinery for working our soil and planting our seeds, but we do hire the big combines to do our custom combining. The rest we do on our own and that's why we go to larger tractors and so, instead of two or three people being out and plowing in the fall, one can go out and plow as much in a day as maybe these two other, smaller tractors. This farm was worked with horses and the first tractor we bought in 1956.

134

"We work in our hay; we run a hundred and eighty-five acres of hay which we start in the last of May and it all goes into bales and we try to have that done by the last week of June. Then this land here, with an average year of rainfall, we can take four cuts of alfalfa. Last year we had the buildings full and we only cut a little, third cut and what could have been the third or fourth cut stayed in the field. And then corn silage, for powdered corn they call it, takes forty-five acres, and then approximately a hundred and thirty acres of mixed grain we use for our own livestock feed and the straw for bedding. I love working with horses but at that time instead of plowing a hundred and eighty-five to two hundred acres you were plowing thirty-five. We have no choice now. There's nothing wrong with it but times change and you're squeezed in on the farm today. The family has to live the same as the people in the city. It's practically the same cost of living only, in the case of the farmer, it's a lot higher. You have to have your vehicles; you may not have your weekends, there's not many weekends off, but you still have to live, so the cost of inflation on our living goes up but our income doesn't go up. So they tell you to increase and be more efficient. And you milk a couple more cows, you milk five more cows to cover that.

"The main part of our concern is our family. My son and myself are partners and my wife helps and we have a seventeen-year-old that's in her last year of high school and she helps on the weekends."

George's father purchased the farm in the late 1920s.

"I like to do the farming with horses..."

Alex McGrath, Killaloe

"This year we worked all winter in the bush and we're still in it. Generally I farm and work out on construction or something but this year is a little different. This year there was a bush sold up the road here to a lumber company and they gave us the job of cutting it out. We don't put up the same amount of stuff as they do with a skidder but we haven't got the expense either. There's lots of guys with skidders right now when logging has gone bad that they could lose them. If they tell us to quit working, well we put the horses out to grass. If they're not working we don't have to meet the payments. If you pay eighty thousand dollars for a skidder you'd want to have lots of work to do. But timber is bad right now. We get a lot of private bushes to cut out just on account of using horses; they don't want to let machinery in there. There's no doubt about it, with the horses you don't knock down the timber you do with a skidder; you use the same trail for a couple of days at a time before you move on.

"I sow whatever crop I sow with the horses. I sow fifteen acres of corn with it and the odd time ten or fifteen acres of oats. I used to do the haying with them but I haven't done any with them lately. I like to do the farming with horses but it's just the time it takes. You have to get back to the bush to make your money. Supposing you have forty or fifty cows on a farm like this, you can't make a living without doing something else.

"The first horses I had I guess I bought from my uncle, when I was fifteen, for ninety dollars with the harness on and I sold them for a hundred and ten and kept the harness. I dealt a lot in horses years back and I still do. I have ten or eleven around here right now but they're not for sale. If there wasn't the horse pulls around there wouldn't be as many horses either. There's a lot of older fellows now would like to have a horse but it's hard to get them broke in on everything, like a wagon. They're just not broke into that anymore. My dad never had more than two or three horses at the most. He sold the odd team but I don't think he dealt in horses as much as I did."

Alex McGrath

Marion and Malcolm Graham

"These are things we know."

Malcolm and Marion Graham, South Mountain

"My grandfather bought this farm in 1885. I've always had a dairy herd. When I came here, in 1957, I'd drive to Kemptville and there'd be milk cans at nearly every gate. Now if I stay on my regular route I pass one other farm on the way to Kemptville. There's not enough money for your labour; you'd make more money working for the government. If other industries and businesses were as efficient and as improved as much as farming, things would be a lot cheaper. In 1905 a farmer produced enough for six people and now each individual farmer produces enough for about a hundred and twenty. We put out of here around twenty-three hundred litres of milk every second day. I don't know how much it would have been in the past. You're producing far more because your input costs are going up. These are things we know. If you decided to be a dairy farmer and hired me to tell you everything, I'd have to stay with you every minute. The things that we know we don't really know that we know. Like my father said when he sold his farm to the doctor's son, 'I never knew how smart I was.' That's why people who come from the city and think they can farm usually have a disaster. There's too many of these little things that they don't know and you can't learn them all fast enough.

"With farming you have to reinvest your money. We've been holding back on reinvesting because this farm is for sale. We sat down and figured out actually what the assets we had were and how much they were worth in market value if we sold them off individually. It comes to a lot of money. So I suppose that is what we'll have to do but then this will never be a dairy farm again, ever.

We decided that it would be easier for us to walk down the lane than have the cows walk down the lane. I've had two farmers tell me that when they made the decision to sell their cows, they cried. And why wouldn't you? I mean we can trace the ancestory of our cows back to 1943, so all of his life the farmer's known them. We don't want to get out but I'm getting to the age were I can't keep going. They say it takes three years to sell a dairy farm and we've only been at it a year."

"He's been getting up at a quarter after five since 1951 and finishing his work at ten o'clock at night and there's been damn few holidays I'll tell you."

Malcolm keeps an eye on his cattle.

"It's her life."

Ron McCoy, Stittsville

"Our kids like the farm here but I don't know if we'll be here much longer because the city of Ottawa is moving out so fast; they're going to push us out. I like farming and I also worked as a farrier. I started working with Clifford Switcher and Stewart Crabb and then I went to Scotland and worked over there. Then, shortly after I came back home and was working here, my dad died. I was nineteen then and I got married and we started farming. Mother did all the milking then and she still does. Then Maureen and I came home and we were doing the chores and shoeing horses and it just got to be too much. We couldn't keep both going; something had to go so the shoeing horses sort of went. We still have a dozen or two dozen pure-bred Belgian horses. We work them and do some logging and do some farming with them. They farmed here with horses up till 1964 and then the drought came in '64 and they didn't have enough to feed all the animals and they had to get rid of the horses. Dad only went two years and then he had another team.

"If people wanted to, if the desire was there and the education and knowledge, you could farm today with horses as efficiently as you could with tractors. When you're working with draught horses you're moving at four miles an hour which is really the optimum speed you can do anything. If you're raking hay and you go much more than four miles an hour you're knocking the leaves off it. Everything in farming works at four miles an hour; that's basically the best speed. If you plow faster than that you are actually causing compaction in the soil. When you are working with horses most of the equipment is either underneath you or beside you or in front of you, instead of behind you. People think that you are talking about going out with a walking plow and plowing; that's not what I'm talking about. I'm talking about using modern techniques, high-speed bearings and things that work smoothly and evenly and not like the old equipment.

"We were showing our cattle at thirteen shows a year. We had a pure-bred herd of cattle and we're a Master Breeders Herd. In 1983 we got the Shield. My dad and mom bought the first Holstein. They didn't have any money but they bought this real good calf. Then my dad went out and bought pure-bred cows and studied up on it all and they went to work and bred up the herd from that.

"I think one thing we have going for us here is my mom. She knows the old ways. She puts in a big garden every year and we're all out there. We do a lot of preserving. She's still in the barn; she's seventy-one years old and she does all the milking twice a day and there are thirty-five cows out there. It's her life."

Maureen, Marguarite, Patricia and Ron McCoy

Clarence gets ready to do some baling.

"You're busier now."

Clarence and Lee Ann Schroeder, Killaloe

"It's just something that I grew up with and it's what I wanted to do. I tried working out for quite a few years before I bought the farm and I didn't like that. Farming is a way of life; it's not just an occupation, it's more than that. It's what you like.

"We need about ten or twelve pure-bred bulls and they're expensive to buy and so we're raising them now. The Charolais, they stay separate and we just raise a few bulls from them. We don't cross-breed them. We have about two hundred and fifty cows and with all young cattle we have

about six hundred head right now. It's getting to be a problem here with the beef business because there's no place where we can sell fat cattle. Slaughter plants are all closed down in eastern Ontario."

"It's just the two of us now. It's the first year our son hasn't been with us. He's always been at home but now he's in Alberta."

"It's a business, it's not like it used to be as a living. You used to just feed your families but now you've got to feed hundreds of people because there's just a few of us. We used to have lots of time to go swimming on Golden Lake and we hardly did anything after supper. My dad raised thirteen kids and we only have one kid and we hardly have a chance to get away. You're busier now.

"I started off in the beef business about twenty-five years ago. It wasn't dairy up here but there was cream. You milked your cows by hand or by machine and separated the milk and you'd sell the cream and then you'd give the milk to your cows. That's the way everybody done it here. We had no cities here and there was no need for the milk business; you couldn't sell it. They wouldn't come down here and get a truck load of milk. This type of country is more suitable for beef cattle."

Clarence and Lee Ann Schroeder

Kathy's father Peter Romme

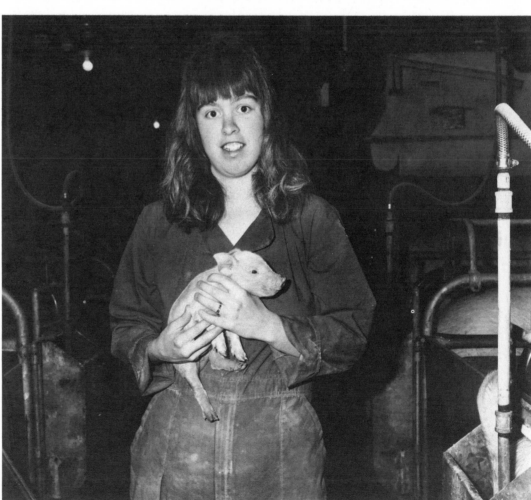

Kathy Bissonnette

144

"I've worked with him since grade eight."

Kathy Bissonnette, Russell

"We have between nine hundred and a thousand pigs in the barn. We sell about thirty pigs a week. My dad was into dairy and cash crop, and then, when he moved here, he was doing just the cash crop. Then he went into beef cattle and then he switched to the pork about ten or fifteen years ago. Beef wasn't making enough money and it was too chancy. He didn't have a big beef operation. I've worked with him since grade eight. I hope to take it over.

"I never get attached to any of the pigs, you don't get a chance. I just purchased one off my dad and that one I go and pet a little bit. They say you should bring somebody in to do the needling and the cutting of the teeth, the hurting part and then you yourself just work with the pigs. If I step into a pen full of pigs they're right away, away from me. They know. The only time I pick up a pig is when it's sick or to needle it or cut its teeth or something. When they're born you have to take their teeth out and cut their tails off. You have to do that or they're ripping the nipples of the sow. If you don't cut the tails, later in life they chew each others tails off and they get infected. They go to market once a week; Dad goes to Finch, that's the Pork Board out there. If we sell wieners most of them go to Quebec.

"This farm is four hundred and ten acres. There's lots of work. I work here four hours every morning steady. You can come in at night and all you have to do is feed and water and it takes a half an hour.

"You average between eight and fourteen pigs in a litter. One sow over here on the weekend had sixteen. The most we've ever had was twenty live pigs, but they never raise that many; they've got fourteen nipples to drink off of so you have to take some to drink off another."

Peter works the fields.

Harold, Keith and Mervyn, the Floyd brothers.

Heading out to the barn to do chores.

"The food was the best part of it."

Keith Floyd, South Gower

"This farm began in 1877. Our grandfather started it. We run a dairy farm here, and we have between forty-five and fifty Holsteins. We start farming at twenty after five in the morning, and we generally get the chores done by seven at night. We started farming with tractors in the fall of 1950. We had a tractor before that, a 1920 tractor, but it was hard times and we couldn't even afford gas to run it. It was a 8-16 International. It would use a gallon of oil a day; it had no oil-pan on it, the oil would just run into the bearings and onto the ground. We used to try and start it when we were young kids. Two of us would get on the crank and try and start it. We never got it going. We traded horses on it.

"In the old days anybody who had ten or twelve head of cattle were milking quite a few. It's quite different taking off a crop now, too. I remember when they used to stook the grain behind the old binder. We'd go out for three weeks in the fall every year threshing. There'd be about thirteen in the gang and it would take us about two weeks, maybe three; generally a day at each place, unless it was a big farm, then it would take two days. The food was the best part of it. They were good meals. These old ladies were good cooks. Mrs. Ellard used to take the pies and take the butcher-knife and make two cuts in them eh, quartered, and set them on the table. They were good cooks, they had lots of experience.

"With a dairy farm you have to be there twice a day, seven days a week. I've never taken a vacation, but I had a week in 1950. I spent a week in Ottawa in the winter of 1950."

Kevin and his father Walter raise fifteen thousand chickens.

148

Jackie and her husband Kevin Kilby, with Walter and his wife Edna Kilby.

"...it has its compensations."

Walter and Edna Kilby, Golden Lake

"We have about forty-five cows and then Kevin has a pig operation and he has about seventy-five sows. Then we started pullets and we have ten thousand pullets in the barn right now and we have a laying operation besides that. The chickens are raised for layers. We raise them from a day old and then they go into a laying barn and they lay for one year and then they're sold to Campbell Soup or the slaughterhouse. Some years beef is not very good, and last winter pork was no good at all and so we like to have something else. We're in the minority thinking that way with so many people just going into milk or beef. The Ministry of Agriculture doesn't believe in that system at all; they think we should have all beef or all pigs. I don't believe them."

"I taught school and for the first few years I continued to teach. I had to work out because we were buying the farm from Walter's mom and dad and they were here too. We needed the money to get started and pay off the farm. The living isn't as high when the two of you work on the farm, until you get well established, but it has it's compensations. You have your free time

149

together and maybe a little bit more time with the family."

"We have four hundred acres altogether. About a hundred and twenty-five is under cultivation and the rest is bush or rough pasture. We brought in twenty-four ton of feed this morning just for the pullets and the laying hens, and for the laying hens that will last a little better than a week. The chickens and the pigs probably go through about five hundred tons a year and that's without anything going to the cattle.

"Most people don't have no idea at all what goes into a farm. That's why we are trying to get agriculture into the classroom. It will give the children some idea why this twenty-thousand-dollar tractor is needed to produce a certain amount of food. I was nervous last year because of the price of pigs. We keep losing two or three

per cent of quota every year and you really need that quota here. But yet you have to keep producing because if you shut down then you have absolutely nothing. And if you do shut down and plan to start up when the prices are better, that's what everybody else does too and so many people come in at once that the prices go back down."

"Farming's not as hard as it used to be. You take threshing, you'd be all day in the barn with the dust and you couldn't see from one end of the barn to the other; there's none of that. You sit on a combine all day. There's more stress but it's not as hard work. You never fork manure; it's all done with a loader. I lived on the farm here all my life and I knew what to do and when, but when you go to school and hear it over again and you get more in-depth reasons as to why you're doing it."

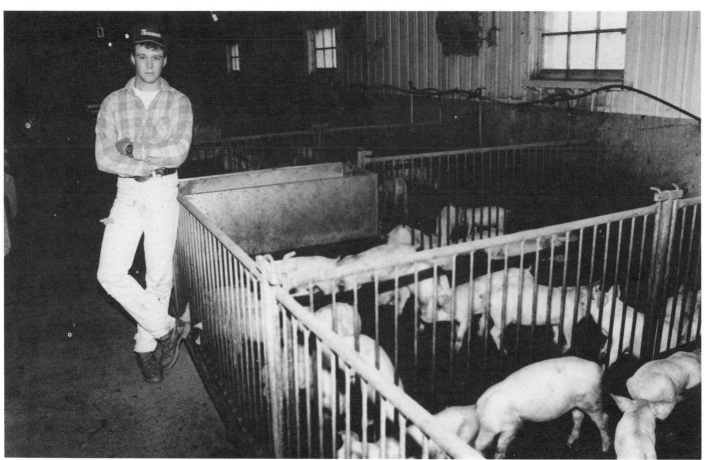

Kevin raises about two hundred pigs.

Alex Hazelwood

"My father needed me at home..."

Alex Hazelwood, Almonte

"We moved here in 1944 and so I would have been six or seven years old. I worked away from home for a while — in Toronto for three years — and then I came back home. I came back for two or three reasons, but mainly because I missed the farm. I couldn't stand the noise in the city. I suppose I was lonesome. It wasn't for the money because there's no comparison. Money isn't a priority any more; I realize that. My father needed me at home too, or he couldn't have continued. My dad and I got along real well. I farmed in partnership with him for fifteen years. I learned a lot from my dad. We had a good working relationship and we could talk about things, about farming and what you might be doing two years from now.

"A farm should be able to support itself and make you a reasonable living. I think we're living in what they call a cheap-food-policy age. For your dollar earned, food has never really been cheaper than it is today. We're at the point right now where I have to decide what to do about the future. Do I encourage my children to do this? They have to want to do it or they'd better not do it. You have to work too hard for the dollar you get. My aim is not only to do a good job but to leave the land better than I got it."

Joe keeps cattle and a donkey or two.

"To be a good farmer you have to like it."

Joe Murphy, Kemptville

"I was born on a farm in Quebec, and the family moved to Ottawa. I was educated in Ottawa before and after the War. I got my degree in engineering. I bought this farm originally on spec. I had two homes in Ottawa, a cottage on the Rideau, and I bought this place when they couldn't sell it. And then, by a series of events, farms across the way became available, so I now have what was four small farms. After I bought the place, my wife decided it wouldn't be a bad place to live, and so we bought five pure-bred heifers in 1958. We've had about sixteen hundred calves born since, all pure-bred Angus. The Angus breed isn't as big as some of these beef breeds like the Charolais or Limousin or the Simmental. A lot of people who have herds of these are now finding they lose a lot of their calf crop — up to ten per cent — in calving because the calves are so big when they're born. An Angus calf is small when it's born, it's hornless, it has a small head, and it grows very quickly after it's born. One of the bulls I had here had a rate of gain in the first year, over a six-month period, of over four pounds a day.

"On the finished end of your raising Angus steers, when you're shipping them out for beef, you'll get a dressing percentage of sixty per cent plus, usable meat on a carcass. Then there is a fifteen-per-cent shrinkage when it's cut and wrapped.

"To be a good farmer you have to like it. Secondly you have to be a businessman, you have to know what you're about. We never have a cross bull here. It's the way you handle them. We don't allow anybody who comes in the place to take canes or electric prods. These bulls you can walk up to and scratch their head"."

152

Joe Murphy

"There's a bond formed between a teamster and a good team."

Bert Timmins, Almonte

"My son has two hundred and thirty-five acres over there where the house and barns are, and I have a hundred acres where there are no buildings. I still farm. We farmed with horses at home when I was young. I didn't have a tractor till I was seventeen years old. I don't really remember starting to drive a horse but I can remember starting to cut hay with the team when I was eleven years old. It was quite a chore to get them in the harness. I had to get up on the oat box to get the collars on them. It was a case of you had to; you were the help. I had the interest in the horses and that was the end that I looked after. There's a bond formed between a teamster and a good team.

"I break a few horses here for people, but I'm thinking about quiting it. I was roughed up a bit last winter. You take a horse that's been shown on a halter, and they're not hard to break because they've been handled. But I get people backing up to the stable-door there and dumping them off and running them into a box stall and they're not even halter-broke. There's no use telling them lads, 'Lets quit'; you're there till it's over. I had a kicker last winter but it was worthwhile. I had one that was a biter, and I really think they're the worst; they're hard to watch. They can take a piece right out. A stallion is the worst to bite as a general rule. Pretty near any horse will test you during the breaking period. Now they might go three or four days or they might go a week, then look out, it will happen. If they're rough when you hitch them then that's genrally the end of it. It's the ones who are meek and mild when you hitch them - you forget about them and that's when the trouble starts. But generally every horse will test you sometime to see if you're going to make them do what you want them to. I find them interesting. Horses get used to you. People drop a horse off here and I maybe harness them or hitch them within half an hour. Well it's all new to them and they're defending themselves; that's what they're doing. I've got to figure out in pretty short order if there's a bit of dirt there and they're ugly, or whether they're just nervous or what's going on. Generally the horses go home in two weeks, broke.

"I hitch a team here everyday in the winter and clean out the beef barn and either draw the manure and pile it, or draw it and spread it. I try and get a horse that's come in here to be broke ready to go in three days and if I can get them on the manure spreader in three days then it's just a matter then of hitching them and driving for a few days and they break themselves.

"I can remember taking cattle to Pakenham. We drove the livestock on the roads to the stockyards. Once we turned out a bunch of steers and got twelve cents a pound for the best ones and nine and a half for the rest. My father came home just on cloud nine with seven or eight hundred dollars. It was about four and a half miles, down the main street and up the hill to the stockyards. Of course by the time they got there their tongues were hanging out and they weren't hard to handle then."

154

Darby with his father Bert Timmins

Alida and her husband Peter Scheepers with their grandson Ryan, son Richard and his wife Donna.

"They came to Canada with nothing..."

Peter and Alida Scheepers, Winchester

"My parents came from Holland in 1952 and the wife's parents came in 1947. My father came as a labourer and worked for an English farmer in Vankleek Hill. When I went to school it was supposed to be French and when I came home it was English or Dutch. My father worked for this farmer for nine months and he was looking for more money and so he found another farmer and got a raise of ten dollars so he went there. I was ten years old and dad started to work at this

farmer's and he went up to eighty dollars a month and he had every other Sunday off. That was fine and it was a decent house and it had a big veranda on the outside. We all came from Europe and we all had little wooden shoes and we were small and we'd run up and down the veranda making a lot of racket and then the farmer said to my father, 'You're fired, them kids are making too much noise.' This was the late fall. My father then hitch-hiked into Ottawa and he started to work for the Experimental Farm."

"They came to Canada with nothing and so did my parents. My father worked for seventy-five dollars a month, with three young children in '47. They gradually built up their own place, starting off with one cow. Then it had a calf the following

Richard and Donna with one of their red and white Holsteins.

year and then you had two. His father used to have a milk truck route where they would pick up milk cans at all the different farms. This is before people got bulk tanks. Peter was the oldest and he had to quit school young and do the field work while his father went and picked up milk cans to have extra income. We have a son there who would like to start tomorrow. But for him to start over and borrow the money at the bank or farm credit or where ever, the interest rates would be too high. There's no way unless he works himself in with his father and gets himself started."

"We have all our own planting equipment and harvesting equipment. You pretty well have to if you want to put it in when it's ready. If you have to wait for somebody sometimes it takes two or three days and you can get awful rains and ruin your crop. We've got three hundred acres and there's too much at stake to wait for somebody else. We have a hundred and fifty cattle and at the present time we milk thirty or better. You milk them seven days a week, three hundred and sixty-five days a year. If you have a party the night before it doesn't matter, you know at four o'clock you have to be there. We're fortunate now we have four boys, we have some that work in town but the oldest son wants to take over and so we get a holiday now and again."

Ray is taking the farm over from his father Clifford.

"They had the very same problems with crops and weather as we have today."

Ray Campbell, Foresters Falls

"I've taken over the farm from my dad. I worked out for three years and so I've had a taste of what that's like and I didn't care for it. I worked in the mine up here and we were working twelve-hour

Ray Campbell and his wife Catherine.

shifts. You'd go in in the morning before daylight and you'd come out and it'd be dark. What we're operating here is four hundred and thirty acres and we're running two hundred and fifty head of beef cattle. You look back over the records, seven or eight years ago, and we were getting the same type of market we're getting now. We're in a situation where you have to take what the other guy is going to give us. It's up to the big meat plants. The last few years we've been shipping straight to Toronto and we find we can get better results in Toronto. We talk to somebody else and he finds he does better someplace else.

"When I was growing up there was chores to do and everything like that. I used to milk cows when I was going to school and dad said if you helped with the chores you'd get a calf at the end of the year. I have two uncles living in Toronto and they were born and raised on the farm here too and they tell me about their experiences years ago and sometimes there's something to be learned from what they tell you.

"Times have changed a lot in some senses but in other ways it hasn't changed. They had the very same problems with crops and weather as we have today. Sometimes the older farmers will tell you some little tricks they learned from the trade and they work today. One old remedy to get a mother to take her calf is to put baby powder on the calf then the cow can't scent the calf and she'll make up with the calf. I never knew that. We tried it this spring and it worked. It was a twin and the mother never took it, so there was another one that lost its calf and it worked with her."

Fern and Carl Bryan

"The dairy is the one that kept us going."

Carl and Fern Bryan, Mountain

"It's been dairy here ever since I was born. Even though milk was a poor price, the dairy was the thing that kind of kept you going. You had the old milk wagon and the thirty-gallon milk cans and you'd take them to the factory. I farmed when I was young and I'm farming now when I'm older. When you're young things are easier than when you get older, although when you're older you have the knowledge to do it easier. Now you get into an air-conditioned tractor and it sure isn't much like using a team of horses. With a team of horses and a walking plow you'd be lucky to get an acre or an acre and a half plowed. Now three or four rounds with the five-furrow plow you have that done."

"My sister married and lived next door and I was visiting there and met Carl. We moved into the farm next door when we were married. I was born just two places down. My brother and I worked together and used the same machinery. I quit school and we farmed together. I got married and we bought this other place and paid a lot of money for it in those days. You didn't have much money to go out and buy machinery, but we were lucky, we had a hen-house there and in '47 and '48 you could make money on hens. We didn't keep too many books and then one year we added up what it cost us and found out we just broke even. So we quit the hen business right there and we changed to dairy. The dairy is the one that kept us going. We worked hard back then. There were people who were better off than others but they didn't show it; there were people who had a good car and we presumed they were out of debt but they worked out in the field the same as we did. They didn't take holidays anymore then we did."

"I smiled when a lot of these government grants came in but on the other hand the young farmers aren't going to farm if they don't get help. In the old days you didn't expect to be a millionaire. I know when I started, I figured that if I got the farm paid for in twenty or thirty years and kept building up that I would be lucky. A good many farmers have maybe four hundred thousand dollars invested. If they had that in the bank at ten per cent they could have a way better life than farming."

Carl, Fern, Carol and David Bryan farm together.

David and Carol Bryan

"A good farm very seldom just happens."

David Bryan, Mountain

"I worked in industry, for two years at Dupont and in Ottawa for a while. When you're on the farm you're not just farming you are in business for yourself and you are doing the work. I think our stress is greater. We have to be able to work. In the summer-time there's very few days that it's not twelve or thirteen hours a day. I was in for twenty minutes for dinner today and I was back out. I wasn't running up and down with a horse, but still on the tractor you're thinking about what you are doing and what you are going to do tomorrow and I might be thinking about next week. I would say in our particular case that it's much harder but I like a challenge and every day is a challenge. It gets discouraging at times but that's part of life. Weather is just one factor.

"I have an advantage over the urban person because I've farmed all my life basically except for about three years when I done the other. Whereas the urban person, they don't get that chance. Mind you it's just as well because most of them would lose it. It's something that has to be bred into you; I really believe that. A good farm very seldom just happens. One of the problems is to try and educate the people who are buying our food about what the problems are. We're not a bunch of half-bakes that throw chemicals on our ground and poison our food. When we put our chemicals on, we put them on ounces per acre. "

162

Orville Faught

"They enjoyed life a lot more."

Orville Faught, Cobden

"I've lived here since 1957. I was born on the next farm just down the side-road. My dad farmed there. I didn't come here from there; I bought another farm up the highway a piece, in 1948. I sold it because this was closer to my dad's farm. We worked together all the time, and it was closer for sharing machinery, and it saved travelling back and forth on the highway. Then eventually I bought my dad's farm too and worked them both together. I have just beef cattle now. We used to milk cows, then we had beef and milk, both, and then we just quit the milking. But the ones that went ahead with the milking, they went into the milking bigger. The quotas are worth more than the farm. To me it doesn't seem right that you have to pay to sell your product.

"They didn't have near as much money back then, but they made a living. They enjoyed life a lot more. When you were working with horses in the field and your neigbour was across the fence, you came up to the fence and maybe your horses needed a little rest and his did too, and so you visited across the fence for a few minutes. When you had the tractor, you never had time to do that. It made it more of a business.

"I always wanted to farm, and I always had it in my mind to farm. When I got married, I bought the farm."

"I think I'll stick with the horses."

Art Ferrier, Perth

"We use horses all winter, drawing manure out and bringing the wood from the bush and I do the seeding with them. I intend to use them raking the hay this year. I'm always trading horses. My father and my grandfather farmed here before me. I have a son, seventeen, and he likes farming but there's so many other things he can make a good living at. He can make as much money going out and working for somebody else than I can here. I always liked horses and I did quite a business in horse-trading for quite a few years. I would trade ten a week. I saved a lot of gas just using them. You use a lot of gas just choring around with small jobs. I think I'll stick with the horses. We had all Belgians and then we sold them last fall and now we have percherons. We showed horses for a few years but there's another thing that got too expensive. Before you go to the fair you have to have liability insurance and now the horses all have to be blood tested and by the time you pay your entry fees you'd have to do awfully well to break even.

"One of the biggest problems on the farm right now is our high land taxes. Our taxes are going up about two hundred dollars every year. They claim these marketing boards are good for the farm, well for every one that makes a success of it, it has put about ten farmers out of business. I think there's only three farmers on this road milking cows now; twenty-five years ago there was forty. We milk cows yet and we separate the cream and sell the cream and then use the skim milk to feed calves; I buy young calves and feed them the skim milk until they're about four hundred pounds and then sell them. There's only two companies buying the cream now. Every Wednesday morning I have to meet the cream truck in Perth. We have a two-unit milker that's forty years old and it works as good as it ever did. We got into cream about six years ago. The field man for the milk board come out and looked around. We were going to have to update all the equipment and we were even going to have to widen the lane, put up fences across the middle of our barnyard so the cattle couldn't get anywhere near the milk house. The field man said, 'Oh for thirty or forty thousand dollars I think you can make this place look pretty compact.' I said, 'I could too, but I'd be milking cows for thirty or forty years to pay you for it.' 'Keep more cows,' he said. On this acreage you couldn't keep more. 'Get more land,' he said. That's how farmers kept getting bigger and bigger — following the government's advice. I didn't do it. We don't owe anybody.

"I can't imagine doing anything but farming, I love farming. I never really liked working for others."

Joan and Art Ferrier

Lois and her husband Mack James.

"...it will be forty years this October since I got her to the altar."

Mack James, Carleton Place

"For me this farm only spans thirty-nine years but for my wife Lois it's a lifetime. The first time we met it was a long drawn-out situation. My father was out west and I was a young lad and I was charged with the responsibility of keeping the show on the road. I was at a threshing over in Huntley and I got word that a herd of cattle were on the road. I had a team of horses and by the time I got the horses home and come over to this area to hunt up the cattle there was no sign of them. In the process I drove into the yard of another farm with a pick-up truck to see if the cattle were back on that property and I got stuck. So it ended up that I was looking for help. So I came over to this place and it belonged to Lois' parents. I was in a pretty bad twist that evening because I had to locate these cattle and my truck was stuck. So I came in here to this house and this pretty young girl was sitting doing her homework and that was the first recollection I had of her. Then we had to get the neighbours to draw me out and by the time I got mobile again my brother came along and we got the cattle. Then it was quite a few years later I was at a Junior Farmers' dance and there was an elimination dance; everyone that had chequered socks they were eliminated and the girls that had bows in their hair were eliminated and it ended up that they couldn't get any way of eliminating Lois and I and another couple and so the way they eliminated it was a wheelbarrow race down the length of the hall. So she had to take me by the heels and we had to paddle along and we raced the length of the hall and we won. So after that evening we got a date going and it took me four years but I finally got her married and it will be forty years this October since I got her to the altar.

"I come from over at Appleton and I was part of the Spring Valley Farms. My dad was one of the first people in the Ottawa Valley to have Herefords. Our family has raised and registered Hereford cattle possibly longer then any other family in Canada, for seventy-five years. He was a boy in the Scotch Bush at Hyndford and he had worked for a man named Sparks and this Sparks man bought cattle and shipped them to the markets in Toronto and Montreal but he also bought cattle and drove them to the farms for the big lumber companies. And my dad was employed with another boy to drive these cattle two hundred miles or so. The shanty men needed the food. They killed the cattle and had fresh meat. He had observed Hereford cattle in these drives of cattle and he observed the odd white-faced animal and he admired them so much that in 1915 he was able to acquire his first Hereford. His first Hereford he bought from a man called Bill Hunter from Orangeville. They are a breed of cattle that has low management and they're an animal that will thrive and survive on poorer pastures. They are the best temperament of any cattle.

"I can remember it being so tough in our household that in order to come up with the little bit of cash to be able to go to town and buy Christmas presents my dad used to load up a dehorning rack on the sleigh and go out through the countryside and cut off the horns for all the cattlemen throughout the country. He didn't always get paid but he got enough out of it to go on that big shopping spree. And they'd have a sleigh load of chickens or turkeys and they used to go to the turkey fair and out of it they'd get cash to get the taxes paid and a little bit of money to buy Christmas presents."

"You learned from your dad."

Eric Beggs, North Gower

"Dad went into jerseys back in the late '30s. They'd take jersey milk at the dairy when they wouldn't take anything else because they wanted to bring up the butterfat. There was a lot of jerseys around here back in the '50s. We were always in the dairy that I can remember and we always sent to Ottawa. We never even had a quota at that time. We could ship all the milk we wanted until the Milk Marketing Board took over. A lot of people think that the jerseys don't produce that much but the top-producing herd two years ago in Ontario was a jersey herd. We have a hundred and thirty head altogether and there's about forty-five milking. We have two young lads and the oldest is talking about going into farming. I would like it if he went and did something else before he tries to farm.

"I didn't go to high school at all. At fourteen I was helping on the farm. I was the oldest son. It was easy to start on your own in them days. You could pick up a rented farm and start out. When they got married the dad gave them four or five cows. You learned from your dad. You were with him all the time. I was ten when we moved up here. I can remember going to a field down on the other place and driving three horses, harrowing the grain field, and dad was in the next field sowing. We worked with horses quite a bit and I still have horses. There was a lot more labour to farming. You didn't have gutter cleaners and the cows went outside to water twice a day. It's still daylight to dark. Now you've got more cattle but you've also got more equipment to work with."

Eric's daughter Donna was the Ontario Dairy Princess in 1988.

Eric Beggs

Dale Gillan

Two staples on a farm: a good dog and a good tractor.

"You have to work out, you don't have the choice."

Dale Gillan, Arnprior

"I've always lived in this area but I only moved here seven years ago. I farmed all my life. I moved here because I wanted a hundred acres all in one chunk; I had land in different areas but there was too much running around. I work out all the time, I've worked out all my life. You have to work out, you don't have the choice. The price of the produce doesn't bring you enough unless you go into it awful large and even then you're taking an awful chance. We don't get much more for our produce than we did ten years ago. The price of our tractors — well seventeen years ago you could buy a forty-horse-power tractor for around forty-five hundred dollars and now they're about fourteen thousand.

"Our kids have all been in 4-H. They did well in it. They'll take over the farm. I wouldn't want to see it sold, that's not a good idea. The 4-H has been great for them, I don't think there's a better thing for kids.

"We don't have the easy way of life that our forefathers had in the way of relaxation. I'm going to take a holiday next week. We had one on our honeymoon and I'll be married twenty-five years next week.

"There are things you may have done differently and you can see your mistakes but I don't think there are any farmers that have any regrets about farming."

Shirley and Earl Saar

"...maybe get better before you get bigger."

Earl Saar, Pembroke

"Agriculture is changing and if we don't change with it we will be changed. Bigger was better all these years from the '60s on and I almost got caught up in that too by building the silos. Then I got to thinking, maybe get better before you get bigger. Shirley and I were milking about eighty cows. We were getting a lot of milk but we were out there three hours in the morning, three and four at night and trying to do the other work in between. Then when my son took over he said we should cull some of them cows. Donald got down to about sixty-five cows and we had more production. We were cleaning up less and we were feeding less. There was less on the expense side and you got more on the income side. I think that's how you get better before you get bigger. Now we've put in four more stalls and we've got automatic take off and almost anybody could milk. It's not how you milk a cow, it's if you leave it on too long, that's where you get the damage.

"We both went up and took over the sawmill twenty-eight years ago. She cooked for me then and we had forty men up there. It was just a sawmill, an office, a sleep camp and a cookery.

Donald Saar works the family farm.

"We sawed logs from about April to October. My dad started a mill here when I was about seventeen and that's what got it into my blood I guess. He started it because there was a big hydro line went through the woods up here and he got a job on there in the winter pulling poles in with the tractor. All these logs were being piled up and so he built a sawmill and people brought their logs and we sawed them all. Then that mill got struck by lightning and burned down. I got out of the lumber business in Algonquin Park in 1970 and came back here to take this over because she was overloaded then.

"I remember sitting up in the office up in the bush there reading the milk act when it came out in '65 or '66. I read that milk act a couple of times and then I got it into my head how that would work. Bill Stewart said: 'This is going to be on farmers if you want it or not. It's going to be a guaranteed thing on the price of your milk. If you give clean milk you will get dollars and they have to take it.' See we were running to Eganville and they'd say we don't want any milk today and then we'd have to run all the ways to Chalk River or Pembroke. Dad used to always draw and haul milk. He always had a big truck and he'd pick up all the farmers' around here and take it into Maple Leaf Dairy. But then that was changing. Big dairies from Ottawa came and bought the little ones."

"The farm is a fantastic place to raise your kids."

Cherry Bekkers, Russell

"We bought this farm in 1966. We were both born in Holland but my husband came when he was ten and I came, with my dad, when I was twelve. When we bought this farm we bought everything. It was a hundred and fifty-four acres and we bought an extra farm adjoining at the back to make it two hundred and fifty acres. There was forty head of cattle maybe on it and the barn was just a small one, sixty feet long, and there was another building there that we tore down. I did everything on the farm except plow. When the kids were small we'd go and bale. I don't know how we did it. We'd bring the kids to the field and we'd put them in a baby carriage maybe in the field. When two of them were old enough we brought them in the tractor. Now that you think back you wonder how did you ever do that. The farm is a fantastic place to raise your kids. Our kids have gone through 4-H and they're in Junior Farmers.

"Farming is a lot of work and it's very stressful because if it rains three weeks in a row, you know you still have to get your crop in and you know you can't get it in. I don't think there's any business that's as stressful as farming because you depend on the weather all the time. And when you have cows, you're just hoping that they don't get sick. It's usually the best cow that you lose and so it is a very stressful business. But it's a very challenging one and it's definitely not boring. I enjoy it but I kind of dislike it on Sundays because Sundays I like it to be a day of family and fun where we don't do any work except what absolutely has to be done. We're lucky that we have a son that's taking over and helping a lot but you still have to be home. We do try to alternate where one Sunday he gets the Sunday afternoon off and the next Sunday we get it off. I often say to my son, 'Why do you really want to farm when you're stuck three hundred and sixty-five days a year where all your friends have weekends off?' But Peter says it would drive him crazy and he likes to farm.

"A farmer isn't necessarily a person in a coverall: he might be a person in a jogging suit, a farmer might be a woman, a farmer might be a person in a suit going to a wedding, but kids at school don't know who a farmer is. I'm sure they think a farmer is a sloppy person in an old coverall."

Cherry Bekkers

Donald keeps an eye on his Holsteins.

"There's a lot more equipment involved now."

Donald Ralph, Kemptville

"My father and mother bought this farm in the fall of '50 and moved in in March of '51. And I guess since I was about seven or eight years old I was in the barn helping. My dad had farmed with his father on the other side of the river. Dad was raised there and he had three brothers.

"We own two hundred and ten acres. Then we rent another seventy acres just a half a mile up the road. We milk on average about fifty cows year-round. There's a lot more equipment involved now. We used to do it by hand. Now the cows are fed by push-buttons and the manure is handled by pushing a button and it goes into a pump and it's pumped out into a storage tank. When dad started, it was the shovel and the wheelbarrow or a litter-bucket and you'd wheel it out and dump it and then later on you forked it into a spreader. But now it's all mechanical. We have a milking parlour. We feed grain in the parlour and the cows know enough when their turn comes, you just open the door and they come in. Once they know, they want to be relieved, to get rid of the pressure off of their udder and they know they get a treat when they get in there. We're into the dairy and we export cattle too, world-wide, and we cash crop a bit of corn. Whatever the silos won't hold, we sell that as a cash crop.

"My son helps on the farm. He's only twelve but he drives the tractors and he can help feed calves. If he wants to get into farming he can but I'd like to see him get educated first. Our farm is big enough we have to have a full-time employee. It's hard to get somebody that cares as much as you do about the business."

Donald Ralph runs a large operation.

Bill Agnew and his brother Tom.

Bill in the milk-house.

"...there's hardly enough days to do it all."

Bill Agnew, Cobden

"I'm the third generation here. It's my dad and my brother and me that work this farm now. My dad is kind of retired but he's still the boss. I remember when I was small we used to milk twenty-four cows, and then we had a bunch of beef cattle too. Now we're milking fifty-five and sometimes sixty, and then we have forty beef cows. There's lots to do. It's a lot of work and it takes a lot of people to get the work done. It's not so bad in the winter, it's in the summer-time, taking the hay off and the grain and the crop and the ripping and tearing. There's hardly enough days to do it all. Like dad says, if you have to hire people, don't bother doing it. Get less cattle and do what you can do yourself. If you hire somebody, a good one, well there's always somebody willing to pay them more money. We just get a summer student to help us with the hay; the hay is the big thing. There's more guys quitting every year.

"I sure wouldn't be farming if I had to buy the farm. I wouldn't borrow the money, sink it all into the farm, work my head off and get zero return; that's what it comes to. A lot of people say that farmers are rich but they have no money. Whatever he makes, he has to put back into the farm."

Dean, Dale, Kevin and Hilliard Boyd

Hilliard and Ruby Boyd

"I bought this farm because I liked it."

Hilliard Boyd, South Mountain

"We moved here in September of '39. Times were tough but we made it through. You start hard but I always liked farming. The sign on the barn with all those names on it, well we have cattle in every one of those countries. They're our Kevlyndale cattle. I bought this farm because I liked it. When we first started here there was a man quit who was a neighbour of ours and I bought all of his machinery, and of course at that time it was horse machinery, for seventy-five dollars, every bit of it. Yesterday I was sitting here on the veranda and they went by with an outfit just to cut and load the hay. There was a tractor and a harvester and a wagon; it was a hundred and four thousand dollars worth of machinery just to do that little bit of work. It used to be that anybody could farm, but not today. I always liked to farm and we made a living here all right and now the boys like it too.

"We never knew how to farm until the Dutch people came over. They had small farms; twenty acres was a big farm there but they use so much fertilizer. They'd buy a farm here and they'd start to use heavy fertilizer and we learned from that. Not only me but I mean everybody. We take off three crops of hay a year. We fertilize the first day of spring and then we fertilize every time we take off a crop of hay."

Dom Coady

"...we've been at the hay since 1960."

Dom Coady, Kinburn

"My dad bought this place in 1947. I was twelve or thirteen years old when dad took me out of school to help him here on this farm. I stayed at home in the summer-time, and worked out in the winter-time. In 1959, I bought half of the farm from my dad and in 1971, I bought the other half. I built up the hay business, and we've been at the hay since 1960. We sold hay then, on the wagon, baled, for twenty-five cents a bale. I store my hay in different barns. We had four boys, plus we hired, and we used to have two balers, two automatic stookers. We used to do around thirty-five to forty thousand bales of hay and straw for ourselves and then we did around twenty thousand bales custom work. Now we generally sell somewhere around fifteen thousand bales. This winter it all went to Florida. The demand down there is for alfalfa-timothy mix, in a mix of thirty-per-cent timothy and sixty-five-per-cent alfalfa. Haying isn't an easy job. It's a hot job, and if you can get somebody to work at it for two or three days, you're doing good. A lot of people have gone to the round bales because they can't get help. There's no way to redo the round bales, to press them and to ship them, they've got to be used here to feed horses and cattle or dairy or whatever. There's less and less square bales made all the time. The less that's made, the better the price for us. I bought a new baler in 1979 for forty-five hundred dollars, and that same baler today is fifteen thousand. Mostly we take two cuts of hay off. We figure the third cut takes a lot of the good away from the plant that it needs for the winter. We really think that you want hay awfully bad to take the third cut."

At the end of a hard day's work.

Albert Storey

The Storey mantelpiece.

"I'm going to stay at farming as long as I can..."

Albert Storey, Kemptville

"I found out the government was going to take some of my land for the highway a long time ago. They only took two acres but the damn trouble is they ruined the rest. I have no drainage. It's been four years now since I plowed a furrow. I have ninety-four acres here now. I was born on this farm and so was my father and my grandfather. We were in the dairy when I was young, such as it was, you know what I mean, but I never liked the milking and I got into beef ever since my parents were old enough to get the pension. I took over the farm more or less when my father died. We were together on it up to that. I expect I'll be the last one on the farm here. I'm here alone and I never was married.

"There's two ways of farming today: if you don't mind owing your soul to the company store or if you're well established. The price of the machinery and the land and everything is so high to start up, and if you want to go in the dairy and the milk quota business that's an expensive proposition. I'm going to stay at farming as long as I can, as long as I can stay on my feet and get going.

"Some of the machinery out there is mine and some of it isn't. A lot of it's obsolete now you know; it's there just for demolition and parts. An old T-50 baler out there was sunk down, away

A farmer's best friend.

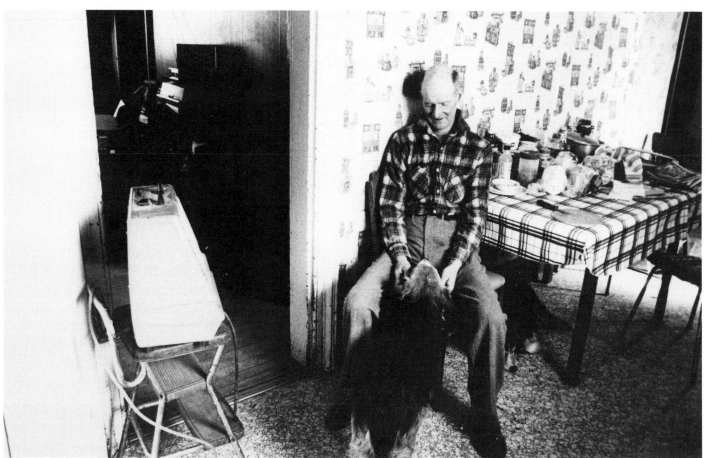

Albert enjoys the company of his dog.

*Albert in his
living-room.*

down in a barn that a fellow was tearing down. He couldn't get it out of there and he wanted it out and he said I could have it if I wanted it. Well actually it's an antique as far as that goes, you know what I mean. The old Case baler of mine, the first one that I had, is out there in that line of stuff there too and there again, it's obsolete. As long as I'm able to work a certain amount I can tear one of them down and rebuild it and offer it for sale and get a few dollars that way. Every time I go to the dump I bring home more than I take. The trouble is, I can look at something and see what I can use something for. It's amazing sometimes, what you can bring home from the dump."

Mark and his father Carl Smith.

Carl is proud of the many farming awards he has won.

"It's big business today."

Carl Smith, Chesterville

"This is a family farm. My father bought it in 1942. As I went up through school we added a little bit more land to it and when I finished school I joined him full time in 1962. We milk sixty cows and we have about a hundred and sixty head of cattle registered. I have one hired hand and a son and myself. We do a lot of embryo-transplant work. We were the first in eastern Ontario to flush a Holstein cow.

"I was in 4-H from twelve to twenty-one years old and then I was a 4-H leader for eighteen years. It helps you learn how to be a leader and to conduct meetings and you meet other people. It helped me quite a bit on the showing and judging of cattle. We specialize in good cattle and this is what takes quite a bit of our time.

"My dad started the farm and there's no doubt about it I wouldn't have the set-up I have today without him. The year I was born he bought this farm. He got a little help from his father and when he started out he had a few head of cattle and a few horses and the like of that. He rented a farm up the road here but he couldn't buy it and so he bought this one and started here. I was very interested in the cattle and I had a good teacher in my father and we worked along good together. We also are good crop people and we keep good crop machinery. We don't buy big machinery but we keep top machinery and we keep it all in the shed, under cover. It's a management deal along with your farming. Not only do you have to have good cattle but you got to grow good feed for them too.

"It's nothing to have eight or ten bus trips in here in a month in the winter-time. I think people are interested in embryos and we're doing quite a bit — flushing of our cattle and selling embryos for export. We've also had great luck selling bulls for stud in Canada. If you keep everything tidy when they walk in the barn then they get a picture in their minds. When they leave they remember your place. But if you have a run-down place they may forget it. It's nothing to have to spend four or five hours in the barn cleaning the cattle up and in the winter-time, their tails are washed every day and they're all brushed off and when visitors come we even take an oily rag and go over them. It's just like when you go to buy a new car, you don't want to buy a car that's dirty.

"You've got to have the basic pedigrees and I think it's probably the cow families and pedigrees in our cattle out here that has really helped us. My father started and then I kept on mainly using great herd sires on our cattle. We buy the odd one but not too many. We try to pick the herd sires from Canada and across the United States that will mate best to one of our cows. Then we're lucky enough that an A.I. (artificial insemination) unit will read about the cow family and if you're lucky enough to have the one that they're looking for well then you'll sell a bull off of that cow. My son now has taken over the breeding end of it. We stuck our neck out and I paid a lot of money for semen off of some of these bulls and it paid off. Like the old saying, it takes money to make money.

"I think one of our biggest and most strongest points about our cattle is that they've got good udders. If you haven't got good udders and good feet and legs you haven't got nothing on a dairy cow. If her legs are bad she's not going to last; she's not going to stand and you don't want these udders hanging way down on the ground and even if they're tied in the barn they're harder to put the milker on and everything and so you'd like to have a good attached udder, up fairly snug, and good feet and legs. We're a little different than a lot of people in that our land is all fenced and in the summer-time our cattle graze. We haul the feed and fill the silo and put in about sixteen thousand bales of hay for the winter but in the summer-time the cows are out in the fields. We figure the grazing in the summer-time helps the cows legs; a cow needs exercise. A cow wasn't meant to be tied up or housed in a small area, they're meant to roam and get exercise. All we feed in the summer-time is grass and a little bit of corn silage and a little bit of high-moisture corn. It's big business today."

Carl outside his barn with one of his prize winning Holsteins.

190

Don Jack, a family friend, helps out on Paul and Amelia, Eva and Barry Yantha's farm.

"We were never hungry..."

Barry and Eva Yantha, Renfrew

"My dad bought this place in '47. I've been running it for twenty-five, twenty-seven years now. He used to help my brother and I, we used to do a lot of custom work. I used to do five hundred acres of combining and maybe a hundred acres of putting in grain and cropping in the spring."

"I was born on a farm up at Bulgers Corners. My parents farmed there. We had a hundred acres and there was eight kids. We lived off the cream cheque and the egg cheque and we sold some pigs and lived off the land. We were never hungry and we had a great life. It's different today, you have to have more of everything it seems, to make money to live. My mother never worked out nor my father and they're both living. None of the lads my age stayed on the farm or anything; I can't think of one around here. My oldest brother went out to help pay for the rest of us coming up. When you work off the farm you know when you're going to get your pay, whereas on a farm you don't know what you lost today or made today. When you get up in the morning you know you've already spent a couple hundred dollars before you even get out of bed."

"The cattle we keep here now are Charolais-Limousin cross. They seem to be a little bit gentler. Any of the boys that are finishing them say they like them because you can put on a heck of a lot of beef on them and they grade well. There's a lot more lean meat on them."

"...it was interesting but too damn much work..."

Ray and Butch Cook, Arnprior

"It's always been a farm. I was running the body shop and trying to run the fire department and there was just too much on the go. Besides there was no money in farming as far as I was concerned. We enjoyed farming. We had a large barn sitting right over there that burned in 1970. We just finished taking in the crop and we got up in the morning and the barn was on fire. I stopped farming about five years ago now. We had a beef farm and we raised pigs at one time. You try and think of things in the future that would make it a bit easier you know, but we got out of pigs. I always felt that if you had a bunch of grain to sell in the fall to the dealers, then you had to go and buy feed, and if you bought seed grain in the spring you only got a third of what you had to pay for it in the first place. So all these things kept getting worse and worse and so I figured it wasn't worth it. You weren't getting what you should have got for it. It's not worth it for a small operator you know."

"The only farmers that make any money today is dairy and they're tied down seven days a week, three hundred and sixty-five days a year. The farmers that is in this area, I can only think of one that don't work out. It seems to be the dairy farmer who can make a better go of it. I got an awful surprise when I was pricing a new tractor about five years ago and I didn't realize they went from nine thousand dollars to thirty thousand. It's understandable how a small-time farmer can't survive if he has to go out and buy a brand-new tractor. If I was to start a farm the only way I could start it is to start it with my dad here because he has most of the stuff here still. Everythings got to be handed down, that's the only way for someone to start out today. I enjoyed when we used to have beef cattle and cut silage and put it in the big silo over there; it was interesting but too damm much work especially when you have to have another job."

Butch and his father Ray Cook.

Murray Hyndman and his father Lanson.

Lanson helps to load one of the heavy horses on the truck.

"...you have to like it."

Lanson and Murray Hyndman, Mountain

"Today it's all mechanized farming; years ago, when I started, it was all labour farming. Everything was done with horses and there was no tractors to load your manure, you did it all with a fork. In milking equipment we milked by hand years ago, now we have milkers that runs the milk into the tank. It's just unbelievable the ways things have changed. We've had a pipeline milker for close to fifteen or twenty years. We milk forty-eight to fifty and we keep maybe sixty cows and then we have a bunch of heifers here. We have three hundred and sixty acres and we rent a little land besides that. This farm has been in the Hyndman name since year one. There's always been a Hyndman lived here. My grandfather and my great-grandfather were all here. I am the third generation to ship milk to Quebec and that boy there will be the fourth. We've never shipped milk anywhere but to Elmhurst Dairy in Montreal. This boy of mine has two sons and he's kind of hoping that one of them stays but I would not say that they would. And you can't blame them too much if five o'clock on Friday they're out and they don't go back to work till Monday morning. We're stuck here seven days a week you know, and I mean stuck. Once in a while you get away and you hire somebody. That's the situation today. There's no big money in farming today. The expense bills are something. I'm not saying that farming, if you like it, isn't a nice living, but you have to like it, you have to like it. And they're selling out fast. There's a big sale right over here today, three miles. The guy didn't have no help and the doctor told him his heart wasn't as good as it might be, so he's just selling the cattle today. That's the way things go. Last fall there was all kinds of men selling out. They'd just maybe get beyond working, some of them, and there's just no labour."

"A lot of farmers got in over their head. A young farmer can't start today. Quotas, so dear, you'd work and work forever and a day and never see the light at the end of the tunnel, never see out. My theory on it is keep your debt low and make a nice living; we make a nice living here, but my wife works too and I have two boys. I feel keep your debt load low and do with a little bit less, that's the way we farm. We just plant corn and grain and hay as our main crop. We make our living out of milk."

"There's nine to ten hours of chores every day to keep us all busy."

Bill and Helen Templeton, Kemptville

"Years ago you worked at everything the hard way, but you seemed to have time to visit. Now everything is push-button and you don't have time. We had a week holiday when we were married and that was forty-four years ago. The way to look at it is that every day is a holiday working on the farm. It isn't a holiday, but you're happy at what you're doing. You get on the tractor and you go out to the field and all you're hearing is the noise behind you. You just kind of block everything out of your mind and watch what your doing."

"There's a lot of people who don't farm who think farming is a pretty boring life in the winter, but we're busier from when the cows go in in November till the end of May than we are in the summer. There's nine to ten hours of chores every day to keep us all busy. You've got a hundred and fifty, a hundred and sixty head of animals that have to be fed, and that's if nothing goes wrong.

"I can recall my dad and mother going down to visit these friends of ours in the States and our friends took them out to see some farmers' set-ups down there. Dad saw one of these stable cleaners work, it was the first one he ever saw, and he was quite impressed with it. When he came home he got talking to me about it and he said: 'It's a wonderful thing when you go and push a button and you just stand back and watch the manure all go out the chute and land in the spreader. You don't have to fork it or use a litter carrier or wheelbarrow or what have you.' So he got a price from a dealer that was just nicely getting to sell these things, Easy Go was the name of it. He came and measured the barn up and it was going to cost us between fourteen and

fifteen hundred dollars to put this stable cleaner into it. That was a lot of money to me and dad said: 'Well, it's like this, I'm getting old and when I stop you'll likely have to have hired help for you can't carry on yourself. If the hired man leaves you at any time then think how nice it will be for you to just push a button and watch the manure go out. You don't have to shovel it yourself or whatever.' Well, he sold it to me just on that. I never forgot that. If you're alone and you have a lot to do how nice it would be just to push the button and watch the manure go out. But today everything has to be done as quickly as possible and you've got to get machinery to do it. That's the changes though.

"Back when I was going to public school the TB test was going through for the first time and my dad had twenty-two or twenty-three cows and everyone of them went down in the TB test except one cow. But when they went down Harry Leacon trucked them all out of here and they all went into the tank. The government had a subsidy but the barn was empty, you might say, that winter. So there came a thaw in February and the water raised on the river just like a skating-rink and my dad hadn't had skates on for a number of years but mother resurrected them from the attic. Of course I was skating a bit at the time and we skated up the river to Mr. Powell's, up Burritts Rapids way on the other side of the river. He said he was planning on selling out his cattle that spring. Dad bought his herd of cows and he was to pick them up in some manner at a later date. Dad was getting pretty tired skating up there and skating home, so we went up to Irwin Lewis', which is the next-door neighbour, and of course they knew them quite well. And Irwin brought us back down the river in the car and dropped us off on the shore. We skated one way and drove back in the car the other way down the river. A couple of weeks later it started to snow, a rough snow, and we chased all the cows down the river and brought them up through the fields there and took them into the old barn."

Robert, Bill, Helen, Matthew, Craig, Nora and John Templeton

"I'm just one of those people who loves a meeting."

Jack Shaw feels as much at home in the boardroom as he does in the barn. And as a regional director for the Ontario Federation of Agriculture he spends plenty of time in both places.

"You want to be able to feel you have determined something about your destiny," says Jack, as he eats cherry ice cream in his Kinburn farm kitchen. "That's one reason I joined the OFA. I was riding on everyone else's coat-tails, picking up on what others were doing for me. I thought it was time to stop free-loading."

No one could accuse Jack of free-loading these days. Since he joined the OFA six years ago, he's taken on one responsibility after another, chaired committees and been the local director. For the past two years he's been the Arnprior regional director, representing two hundred and seventy farmers in the northern parts of Lanark County and Ottawa-Carleton and the southern part of Renfrew County.

"The Federation in itself isn't political; it's a lobby group but not partisan by any means. It gives the grass roots the power of lobby and that's what it's all about," says Jack.

Over the past six years, Jack has become a strong local lobbyist himself. With support from the OFA, he helped to get farm taxes reduced in his township of West Carleton. He led a group of eighty-eight West Carleton farmers and landowners who raised twenty thousand dollars, took their case through the courts and succeeded in getting each property assessment reduced by as much as twenty thousand dollars. "It worked out well for everyone," says Jack.

Nowadays Jack is trying to persuade West Carleton council that a soon-to-be-abandoned Canadian National Railway line should be returned to the adjacent landowners and farmers.

As well as his local concerns, Jack attends monthly provincial OFA meetings in Toronto where everything from farm-tax rebates to the Canada-U.S. Free Trade Agreement is discussed and often acted upon. "I enjoy having a say in what happens," he says.

When he's not attending meetings, Jack, his wife Audrey and sons John and Scott run a six-hundred-and-twenty-acre Holstein farm just east of Kinburn, close to where Jack's ancestors first settled in 1855. The couple's daughters, Donna-Lee and Jill, live close by.

The family milks fifty-five registered Holsteins, shipping fifteen hundred litres every second day. They also have seventy Holsteins in their breeding operation. The family grows corn, hay and grain, though they sell very little. "We see the cows as our conversion unit," says Jack with a wide grin.

Shawhaven farm sits on John Shaw Road, named after Jack's uncle who still holds the local record for involvement in municipal politics. Following his uncle's example, Jack has been heavily involved in the community since he was a young man. He was a township councillor for six years and reeve for one, and he was chairman of the design and building committees for the Kinburn Community Centre. "I'm just one of those people who loves a meeting," Jack says.

"If you don't like something, I always say, join an organization because you can't do anything from

Scott, Audrey, Jack, Helen and John Shaw

An OFA supporter.

the outside. The OFA has a direct impact financially and their large membership gives us a lot more political clout," says Jack.

Twenty-two thousand farmers in forty-six county and regional federations come under the umbrella of the OFA. Another twenty-six farm-related organizations, representing marketing boards, commodity groups, educational institutions, co-operatives and other rural service groups, also belong.

The OFA's widely based farm membership brings credibility to its historic purpose: Farmers working for farmers. Its roots date back to 1791 though the present name wasn't adopted until 1940.

For one hundred and thirty dollars a year, OFA members receive services such as health and life insurance. Each region and county also has its own OFA field representative who helps farmers deal with specific problems such as fence disputes, and supplies them with the information they need to be more effective farmers. Farm and Country, the OFA's newspaper, also helps them to be better informed. But, according to Jack, the most important aspect of the OFA is its power of lobby, locally, provincially and, through the Canadian Federation of Agriculture, nationally.

Over the years, the OFA and CFA have helped to bring about a wide variety of legislation and programs to help farmers including tax breaks, assistance to new farmers, reduced licence fees, farm-fuel rebates and soil conservation programs.

One of the Federations most successful efforts was its involvement in setting up and encouraging marketing boards. "I remember when we started farming here in 1957 we were getting about three dollars and fifty cents for a hundred pounds of milk. The Milk Marketing Board has been a real plus," he says.

"Why produce for a surplus? Why should consumers pay for storing milk powder or butter, or dumping it on the world market? With milk marketing you produce to need."

Jack says that he would like to see more supply management and he discounts farmers' fears that they will lose their independence. "It doesn't matter who you work for or where you work, there's always someone above you telling you what to do. Marketing boards have given power back to the farmers. We have local representation and we have a cash flow too. I think supply

management is the greatest thing since sliced bread," he says.

But Jack is concerned about the future of Canada's supply management. He fears that the Canada-U.S. Free Trade Agreement might open the borders to less-expensive U.S. agricultural products.

"I wonder how long we'll have the power to set our prices under free trade. We can't compete south of the border with our climate, but farmers were such a minority it didn't really matter what we thought about free trade. It didn't count. It was devastating for the grape growers in Niagara," says Jack.

He thinks farmers have to unite in order to obtain the power they need to fight free trade and other problems. "Whatever the organization, whether it

Farmers throughout the province are proud to show their membership.

be OFA or NFU (National Farmers' Union) or the Christian Farmers' Association, I really don't care, but I think you should have one organization which represents farmers," says Jack. "I'm against smoking, but I support the tobacco farmers. We have to support each other."

Sitting on the OFA's environment committee, Jack sees firsthand one example of the infighting between farmers. "Right now there seems to be a lot of concern between mainstream farming and organic farming. We need some sort of co-operation between the two groups so we recognize those who wish to farm organically, but also point out that what we're doing isn't detrimental to the environment," says Jack. At the root of that problem, Jack says, is the public's perception that mainstream farmers use too many pesticides.

"Farming has changed," he says. "I remember when we sprayed and we didn't wear gloves, we didn't wear masks — things that never should have been done but were done. It's certainly different now."

By 1991 everyone who handles pesticides will have to be licensed: Jack and his son John already are. "Not only are you looking after the environment, you're looking after yourself. The land is our future and our own health is our future. There's certainly been a great change in agriculture to make us environmentally conscious."

But, Jack laments, the public isn't aware of this change. "We're poor marketers. We have a terrible reputation and it's our own fault," he says. "The OFA has twenty-two thousand members and we don't have the budget to have a marketing department. We really should."

The OFA now spends money on television advertisements, supplies books for school libraries, and takes part in agricultural displays. "We have to educate the public if we hope to keep our place in society. We have to gain their support. We're down to something like three per cent of the population so we really don't mean anything politically, but if we can educate the general public and make them aware of what is happening it is to our advantage," says Jack.

Jack takes the image problem one step further; he'd like to find a new word for farmer. "I would like to come up with a better description. Elsewhere, terminology has changed, it's been updated. You aren't a treasurer, you are director of finance. The word farmer is obsolete now," says Jack.

Chapter Four

After the Day's Work

"We keep Castleford alive."

Doris Ferguson figures that she has been involved in the Castleford Women's Institute for at least four decades. She remembers attending her first meeting shortly after she married Bob, half a century ago.

"It was the only way you got to know people then. It was a tradition. Everyone did it," says seventy-four-year-old Doris. "It was pretty secluded when I first moved out here."

Doris' daughter-in-law Margaret, who comes from the town of Warren in northern Ontario, has been a member for about twenty years. "The Women's Institute helped me to feel at home. It was like joining a big family of wonderfully warm people," she says. "I've learned a lot."

Doris and Margaret run a one-hundred-and-forty-five-acre beef-cattle farm with their husbands, Bob and Doug. Doris says that when she joined the Castleford Women's Institute, all the members were farmers. That's changed now, at least in Castleford, where fewer than a third of the twenty members work on farms. Despite the changing membership, the basic purpose of the Women's Institute has remained the same - to educate and provide social opportunities for rural women and to make their community, country and world a better place in which to live. It's a pretty ambitious agenda but it translates well to a local level.

The Castleford Women's Institute is one of seventeen in the Renfrew district. Castleford is a distinct six-kilometre area along the Ottawa River, marked by an Institute-maintained park, complete with a Canadian flag and historical plaque honouring Castleford's founder Christopher James Bell.

The Castleford Women's Institute began in 1913, just sixteen years after the Women's Institute was co-founded by Adelaide Hoodless and Erland Lee in Stoney Creek, Ontario. Adelaide decided that educational programs for rural women were necessary after her baby boy died from drinking unpasteurized milk. Today, the Castleford Institute is part of a forty-thousand-member international organization which prides itself on being non-sectarian, non-partisan and non-racial.

This third Tuesday of May, thirteen members of the Castleford Women's Institute occupy every available seat in Mary Ferguson's tidy home on the River Road. They sit in the kitchen and adjoining living-room, chatting with their neighbours and friends and taking care of the business of the day - not just their Institute's workshops, projects and fair exhibits but a wide range of national and international issues which affect home and country.

The Institute Code sums up the feeling that binds the group together:

A goodly thing it is to meet
    In friendship's circle bright,
Where nothing stains the pleasure sweet
    Nor dims the radiant light,
No unkind word our lips shall pass
    Nor envy sour the mind,
But each shall seek the common weal,
    The good of all mankind.

The meeting begins with various announcements: three hundred dollars has been donated to the Renfrew Victoria Hospital expansion project; a new leadership-skills training program is announced; the Tweedsmuir local-history entries are due in September; the Federated Women's Institute of Ontario's child-care questionnaires will soon arrive; a thank-you note has been received from the Renfrew and District Food Bank. The women vote in favour of a landscaping seminar. Members give Pennies for Friendship, money which goes to the Institute's international counterpart - Associated Country Women of the World - for a wide range of projects from well digging in Africa to international conventions.

This is Averil McLeod's first meeting as president of the Castleford Women's Institute. Averil is a relative newcomer; she joined eight years ago. "You're not long in the Women's Institute before you get some work thrown at you," she says with a smile. "The most important thing is to get involved."

It's difficult not to get involved. The Castleford Women's Institute has twenty-one positions, executives and conveners whose concerns range from international affairs to visiting community members who are ill or house-bound. Both Doris and Margaret have taken a turn as president. Doris, the Institute's oldest active member, says she thinks she's held every position except those of treasurer and secretary; Margaret has held them all. Margaret says that it has really helped her to gain self-confidence.

"She wouldn't even go to a meeting at first, if I didn't go too," says Doris.

"There's lots of things I'd do now that I wouldn't have tackled before," says Margaret.

This year, Doris is the Public Relations Co-ordinator. She writes up the Institute news for the The Renfrew Mercury and she also

encourages people to join, and sends cards to local people who are sick.

Margaret writes letters to the Institute's foster-child in Liberia and is also the Institute Convener for Citizenship and Legislation. She has the gigantic task of monitoring new government legislation and determining its effect on family and consumer laws. "I try to figure out the effect locally," she says.

This monitoring sometimes leads to a local resolution seeking change. These resolutions can rise through the ranks to the district, provincial and sometimes national Women's Institute and may result in changes to legislation. Locally, the Castleford Women's Institute is lobbying to get better signs for their community on Highway 17 at County Road 20. Members successfully lobbied Bell Canada for private lines to about one hundred Castleford homes and cottages. Residents used to pay an average of twenty dollars extra each month if they wanted a private line; now the service is free.

Provincially, the resolutions of the Federated Women's Institutes of Ontario helped to bring about legislation requiring bread to be wrapped for sanitary reasons. Years ago, bacon packages had red lines on them, making the product appear to be leaner than it actually was — the provincial Women's Institute had this banned. The organization has lobbied to have white lines painted on roads, to have hot meals, medical inspection and musical instruction in public schools, and to set up libraries and medical clinics in rural areas.

Federally, the Institute has lobbied for an improved Canada Pension Plan for women, for controls on TV violence and obscenity, for better

The Castleford Women's Institute meet in Mary Ferguson's home. Margaret Ferguson is seated on the right in the front row and her mother-in-law Doris is in the second row at the left.

waste management, and for quicker reimbursement for thalidomide victims.

These broad concerns are important, but the Castleford Women's Institute members also concentrate on educating themselves and looking after the community.

"The meetings are mainly to keep the community together," says Doris. "If we don't have them, the community grows apart."

As Margaret puts it: "We keep Castleford alive. We're Rural Route 5, Renfrew, now, not ourselves. We give the area an identity."

The members keep a record of local history and in 1986 they published Horton: The Story of a Township, as a fund-raising activity and to celebrate their local heritage. The Institute also raises money through bake and quilt sales.

The money lets the Castleford Women's Institute sponsor its own high-school scholarship program,

Proud to be a member.

and donate money to local projects including a local home for battered women, the Renfrew Food Bank and the Ottawa Cancer Lodge. "If there's a fire, we try to help the family too," says Doris.

Improving the home-making skills of its members is an important part of the Institute's activities. Members represent Castleford at the Renfrew Fair with an annual exhibit of home-making arts. This year's theme is a "Child's Paradise." Margaret is making a bib and Doris has promised a bottle-warmer and a child's quilt. "I like the crafts and sewing best," says Doris. "We also provide leaders for 4-H home-makers and I've taught lots of girls to sew. One of them made her wedding dress in our class and she wouldn't show anyone until she showed me. I thought that was cute."

Doris is also an expert quilter and through the years she's led many Institute workshops. "Some are all left-handed. Sometimes I bet I had to do half the work over again. We had a lot of fun about that, but we all tried."

Margaret says she likes the cooking programs best of all. "I've been baking bread for twenty-five years and you'd think I'd know everything but I don't really. I learned how to avoid air bubbles during a course a little while back."

Members decide which courses their Women's Institute will offer. Gardening is a current favourite. At the May meeting, members answered the roll by presenting a cutting or seeds to share with the group. But farm courses are quite rare. "Over the years we've had courses on farm safety and first aid and safe machinery practices, but there isn't much demand right now," Doris says.

There is now a Women's Institute movement to get agricultural instruction back in the schools. The provincial organization wants to see the well-known Ross Butler pictures of farm animals used in school instruction. Institute President Averil says, "There's a real gap in agricultural education at the schools."

Despite, or maybe because of all the programs and activities, friendship is a basic component of the Institute.

"Everyone talks about how peaceful it is in the country, but with the number who come to the door and telephone, we're never lonely or bored," says Doris.

Mildred and Norm Adams

"We're as busy as we want to be."

Norm Adams, Bishops Mills

"I was born and raised on the farm. My brother and I farmed after my dad and mother passed away. We owned a general store and it was a very busy life running it. My brother kept the farm for a while and then he sold it.

"I've played the fiddle for quite some time. I've always been interested in music. Mother played the organ and my dad played the fiddle some. On Sunday night mostly everybody was at home and mother would play the violin and we would sing by the hour. There was no real problem to get the family to do this. We sang a variety of music; mother had songs that she sang, as well as gospel and just a variety. When we were in the store, we didn't have time to play. I'm in a band called Grenville County Country and we played last Sunday morning for the United Church anniversary service and we play for wedding receptions, wedding anniversaries and dances. We're as busy as we want to be."

Some of Norm and Mildred's favourite music.

Norm and Mildred play a few tunes.

"...we played there till the mortgage was paid off."

Clarence Williams, Carp

"I used to play in a country band and they had this thing called a broom dance in the old house parties years ago. A couple would catch two brooms and they'd start dancing with them and then everybody else would start to dance and when the music stopped they threw the brooms down and then grabbed their partner. It just started as kind of fun. I learned to play the piano and the guitar at the same time, the year I was fourteen. My father played the fiddle. We used to go to house parties down by South March and then it progressed through the years. I remember the first night I played I got two dollars. I played for a wedding reception down by South March. I played at the Perth Legion for ten or fifteen years. We did country music and old-time waltzes and sang. I had a lot of fun with it. We played the first dance that was in the Legion at Perth, Jim White and us, we played there till the mortgage was paid off. We were there every Saturday night. We never had a bad crowd, always a good crowd and some nights it was packed full. I had a heart attack in '79 and I quit playing, and I've never played since. The first three months or so after that, God it was a long Saturday night.

"They let the farmers go broke all over the country because the lads in town don't want to have the price of hamburg go up. The feedlots are all broke in the country and the farmers are gone. Back of the road here there's three farms gone because the government didn't want to pay for their cattle. The banks get their big money from the interest and they keep putting the interest rate up. The money goes to the middleman and the farmer doesn't get anything. You have a place like here and you can't even make a living on it. My father bought this place and another place for a pasture lot down on the Ninth Line and the place across the road, a hundred acres there. He rented my uncle's hundred acres beside it and he raised three kids and had a hired man. He paid for all the other places on a hundred acres. Today you can't live on a hundred acres unless you have a job in the city or in town.

"I get a kick out of when the calves are born. I remember my father was the same way. Every spring he'd look forward to the cows calving and you'd get the first calves coming and they're so quiet. The last thing at night he used to go with the old lantern and check all the cattle, and I guess that stayed right down with me because I used to do the same thing and I do the same thing at night yet. I take the flashlight and walk out to the barn and listen to the cattle grunting and they're all lying there so full and chewing their cud. We used to milk and cream separate and fifteen years before he died he quit separating. We had a milking machine, a little outfit that Canadian Tire sold, and it had two glass bottles on it and it would run with a gas engine and you'd run it along behind the cows and it worked like anything. This was back just before the War. It was the simplest outfit, a natural milker. I don't know where they come from or where they disappeared to. It was two hundred and some dollars. I did all the milking the full way down the barn every day. It was all timed at a certain speed and you'd crank it up in the morning and crank it up at night and the cows, it didn't bother them a bit, they just sat there chewing their cud."

Clarence Williams

The Royal Black Perceptory is the highest order in the Orange Lodge. These Richmond members meet once a month. Many Ottawa Valley farmers belong to the Orange Lodge.

The inside of the Orange Lodge in Richmond.

This Richmond Ladies Orange Benevolent Association has been meeting regularly for thirty-five years.

215

Basil Hodgins

Eric and Evelyn Campbell, Betty Cameron and Basil Hodgins have put out three tapes of their old-time music.

"A country boy, that's all I am..."

Basil Hodgins, Bristol

"Eric and Evelyn and Maye and I have been chumming together for a good many years, I don't know, maybe twenty years. But to get together and make a tape or anything like that, it's been just the last few years. I learned to play the harmonica on the clothes-line stand at home. My mother didn't want me to play it in the house, I was making too much noise. She had eleven kids so I guess she was quite glad when I'd go out on the clothes-line stand because I think she had enough noise without me. I like any kind of music that tells a story. I don't feel a song is a song until it tells a story. That's my way of thinking and I don't mean I'm right. I record all my music in my head and then put it down on tape. I mostly do it when I'm on the equipment, either the truck or the grader, and if it sounds good then I come home and I try it out on the wife. And if she don't kick me out I know it's not too bad. I like my first song I put out called 'True Country Livin'' because it takes me back to my childhood, and my parents are involved."

True Country Livin'

Back home in the country,
When I was just a lad,
Luxuries and fancy things,
My parents didn't have.

We didn't have no TV,
We had no video games,
A radio was all we had,
To keep us entertained.

We didn't have no telephone,
We had no electric lights,
A coal-oil lamp was all we had,
To help us through the night.

We didn't have no fancy car,
To help us get around,
A horse and buggy was all we had,
To take us into town.

In the evening we would gather 'round,
And Mom would make us toys,
And out of wood my Dad would whittle,
With all his pride and joy.

For a farmer he would file a saw,
Or make an axe handle out of wood,

Oh we didn't have much money,
But we did the best we could.

When Saturday night rolled around,
We'd go to the general store,
A nickel to spend was all we had,
And not a penny more.

Some kid would buy a licorice pipe,
And some an ice-cream cone,
But me, I'd buy Cracker Jacks,
So I could take 'em home.

A country boy, that's all I am,
And that's all I want to be,
Where the air you breathe is nice and fresh,
And the grass is nice and green.

And the neighbours they all greet you,
With a nice friendly smile,
Come on in and sit right down,
And chat with me a while.

We didn't have no wacky-tobaccy,
We had no LSD,
But in our home we had a lot of love,
In 1943.

Basil and his musician
friends play a few tunes.

Members of the Richmond Quilting Bee, Mary Lalonde, Betty Peacock, Alice Dupuis, Evelyn Vaughan and Ann Spratt, work on a quilt.

"We each do a square."

Ann Spratt, Richmond

"We've had a quilting bee for five years. We have six members. We started it here, in the basement, just two or three of us. We made one for the library and one for the Legion from pieces we already had. That's the old-fashioned way, just use the pieces of material that you have. We do traditional quilts. A lady wants one in the fan pattern that she's going to raffle. I think in a group, we get along better doing an appliqué one. We each do a square. It's just a fun thing.

"I've been quilting since I was a kid. My aunt taught me. I like the more intricate patterns. I belong to the bee, but I still do ones on my own. I give them to my family. I made one for my sister-in-law. I still have my mother's treadle machine. I don't use it, but it runs like a top."

"...practically every house had a fiddler."

Gib Bennett, White Lake

"I started to fiddle when I was about twelve years old. The first song I learned was 'Jingle Bells'. I joined the Renfrew County Fiddlers about five years ago. We travel around quite a bit.

"Years ago, some families were all dancers and all musicians. They were all farmers. All these house parties were all farm homes; they didn't have them in the villages, as a rule. It was lots of fun. At one time, practically every house had a fiddler. There was no trouble to go to a wedding reception, get three or four guys up that knew one another real well who could all play together. When there were wedding receptions

all you did was make sure there was somebody there to start it. Most of the fiddles were bought in Eaton's catalogue."

Gib on his front porch.

Gib's fiddle is never far away.

Gib Bennett

The Perth and District Old-Time Fiddlers have been getting together every month for the past twenty-three years. The group's executive includes Arnold Darou, Bill Buffam, Phylis Dodd, Winona McDonnell, Lindsay McDonnell and John Camelon.

Round dancing at the Perth Legion.

Calling a square.

Everyone comes out for the St. Patrick's Day Dance.

Many musicians play during the monthly dances.

Clarence Barrie strums a few tunes during the Perth and District Old-Time Fiddlers' St. Patrick's Day Dance.

Martin has been playing the fiddle since he was a young lad.

"A real gift he had."

Martin Felhaver, White Lake

"My uncle is a pretty good fiddler. I always liked the fiddle. I can remember a long time ago, when I was just a young lad, they had a dance at my place, and a neighbour of ours, who was a good fiddler, came and sat on the chair, and well sir, I never got over the way the old lad could play the fiddle. That rang in my ears for days after that.

"I lived in Arnprior, and I worked for Gillies all my life. When I was about seventeen years old, I went to the lumber camp. I spent about eight or ten years in the lumber camps every winter, and then I came down here and I drove the locomotive in the lumber yard for about twenty years. There was a lot of farmers in the lumber camps in the winter. His wife and family used to look after things. There was a lot of farmers that did that. We used to call them habitants. They'd bring their own team in there after Christmas, for the sleigh haul. They'd quit sawing logs and they'd draw out, skid out and draw them out on the lake or the river.

"There were lads that used to play in the lumber camps when I was there. They'd play mouth organs and that, eh. And I used to know all their tunes. I never took my fiddle up to the bush. At one time there was a real good fiddler there. He come into the lumber camp kind of late. He was a big, tall fellow, a French fellow; oh, a very nice lad. He came out to roll, and he didn't know how to roll or nothing, and so I showed him and helped him, and after he was there a few days, he used to whistle and, Holy God, he could whistle tunes. I said to him, 'Can you play a fiddle?' 'Oh yes,' he said, 'I can play a fiddle.' He said he hadn't played for a while because his dad had died. So there was a lad in the camp and he had a fiddle, so I went over to him and said, 'Look that French fellow there said he can play the fiddle; will you loan me your fiddle?' 'Well sure,' he said. Well that French fellow started to play French tunes you know and the feet going, Holy God, it was nice to hear him playing. A real gift he had."

Martin Felhaver

Campbell MacLaren

Most days, you can find Campbell on the front porch with his dog.

"...it's the only real music there is."

Campbell MacLaren, Cobden

"The old dances were fun. I played the fiddle for years at dances. I played all night and never get a cent for it. It was all for fun, everybody went for fun. I had three uncles who fiddled and so I bought one when I was a young lad and I learned to play a little bit. I never was a musician but I had a lot of fun with it. As far as I'm concerned it's the only real music there is. There was a good many dances right where we are sitting here; there'd only be about two dozen at them but they had a lot of fun. Everybody knew everybody else. There was always somebody who could sing or tell a few jokes to keep the thing going. They went till two or three o'clock in the morning. Lots of times I came home and changed my clothes and went to the barn to milk the cows. There was old people and young people and everybody else at them parties.

"Everybody's in too much of a hurry today. Today you have to buy everything. It used to be that when you had a job to do you called in one of your neighbours and he'd help you do it and you helped him do something. Thirty years ago, in 1960, my out-buildings were burned here. I lost sixteen cows that were milking and the young cattle were still outside in the yards. That left me with about thirty-nine head of cattle after the fire and nothing to feed them in November. I didn't have enough materials to build again but I had a good bush on another farm and the neighbours helped me. I went to the bush and cut thirty thousand feet of lumber and got it trucked out to the sawmill and sawed. Then a bunch of the neighbours drove in and helped me truck the lumber home and pile it. We started to build the barn in the spring of '61 and I had another barn built and ready for haying. I hired two men and every day there was half a dozen men came in from all over the country to help. They were all local farmers from Portage to Osceola. For three days in a row there were twenty-two men working on the barn. If they had a day to spare they'd come out and give me a hand to put the barn up. That kind of thing is all changed. Today you'd have to hire a contractor to give you a price on how much he was going to charge you to build a barn."

A memorial dedication at the White Lake Women's Institute.

In memory of those faithful members
Who served for Home and Country well
We recall each one in sacred measure
Those who have passed beyond the veil

Lucila Jones

Members are proud of their Institute hall.

230

Members from neighbouring Institutes join the White Lake women at a social tea.

It was the White Lake Women's Institute's seventy-fifth anniversary in the summer of 1990.

Hugh and Mary Lunney

"The Old Apple Tree"

Hugh Lunney, Pakenham

"I've lived here all my life. A lot of people move quite a few times in their lifetime, and all I say is, all I ever moved was when I got married; I moved from one bedroom to the other, to the warmer side of the house. We milked cows all our life till last year when we sold our milking herd. The milking always, and certainly in the later years, was the main thing for the whole farming community; it was a guaranteed income. You had to have a quota, and you had to send so much milk, but you knew exactly how much you were going to get each month. Whereas beef, you never were sure what you were going to get.

"I was always the one that liked the horses the best and generally, when you like something, you're pretty good at it. It wasn't long before my mother would trust me more in driving the horses than my father. I drove the old cars, but I'd sooner have the horses. I could live in the old era. I'd be quite happy to work with horses.

"I like telling stories, and I like singing, and I like dancing. But like telling stories the best; here's 'The Old Apple Tree.'

Hugh with his favourite team.

"Maggie Jones she was a homely maiden,
And Maggie owned a homely apple tree.
Sweet Maggie's face was covered all over in
freckles you see,
To tell the truth she's homelier than me.
I've never called upon the fair young damsel,
Until one day I was passing by,
She said if I would pick for her some apples,
For me she would make an apple pie.
So I climbed up the old apple tree,
For the pie was the real thing with me.
There was Maggie below,
With her apron hung so,
Just to catch all the apples I see.
But just then a limb broke.
Holy gee, I fell from the old apple tree.
I broke some bones,
And nearly killed Maggie Jones,
In the shade of the old apple tree.

"Well, my dear old father, he was quite a fighter,
And mother she was quite a fighter too,
Especially when fighting with poor father,
She used to pound him till he was black and blue.
And father would find a soft spot in the wood shed,
To try and sleep his little jag away.
But there's one thing about my dear old parents,
In the house they never fought, that I could say.
They'd go out beneath the old apple tree,
Where they'd have much more room,
don't you see,
Then ma she'd butt in,
With a big rolling-pin,
And pound pa till he couldn't see.
In this hustle they upset the beehive,
And they found that the bees were alive,
For the bees they stung ma,
And they stung the hell out of pa,
In the shade of the old apple tree."

Headin' down the road.

"Up the elm and down the pine, You swing yours and I'll swing mine."

"And 'round again," calls Dave Duncan over the reel of fiddles, drums, guitar and piano. There are already nine squares bobbing and swinging, any more and they'll have to move into the kitchen. It's the March square dance at the Pakenham Community Centre and they're turning them away at the door.

When Dave started calling forty-five years ago there was a dance pretty nearly every night. It's not like that any more, but in Pakenham the Burgess and Duncan families lie at the heart of a local revival. They are a closely knit clan. There's Dorothy and Dave Duncan, and Dave's sisters Lillian and Irene who are married to brothers, Ross and Ernie Burgess. Dave's niece, Monica Burgess, started the Wednesday-night square-dancing club in the fall of 1987. It now has about forty regulars, making five squares. And the monthly dances attract people from as far away as Perth and Ottawa.

It's hard not to have fun square dancing.

235

Tonight, Dorothy is the dance go-fer, she helps prepare the midnight lunch and minds the lights — you need everything blazing to avoid a tangle of feet and arms during a square. Dorothy has been dancing since she was eleven and fondly remembers her courting days, dancing to Charlie Finner's Hay Shakers Orchestra. She first saw Dave when he was calling at a Junior Farmer's dance. He won the contest and Dorothy still considers him to be one of the best callers around. Not surprisingly, all six of their children square dance. At a wedding they form a family square.

Wilbert Munro, an eighty-year-old retired farmer from Clayton, says that he's been doing squares for sixty-five years. "I got married fifty-six years ago and two weeks after I got Florence home, I got her square dancing," says Wilbert. By way of explaining his passion he says, "You get used to it." The Munros used to take their five children to the square dance every Saturday night.

Dave, who started the monthly dances, is one of five callers on hand this blustery March evening. "I was surprised how well it went. We've had a grand turn-out right from our first dance, back in April 1988," says fifty-nine-year-old Dave. Today the dances routinely sell out, all two hundred and fifty places. "There are lots in our age group sitting around with nothing to do. This is something for them to get out to. They were raised on this old music."

Dave was raised on it too. He's been calling since he was fourteen years old although there was a time, during the '60s and '70s, when he didn't — he was too busy raising children, milking his forty or so Holsteins and tending his forty-four-hectare farm, Madawaba, at the junction of Waba Creek and the Madawaska River. He retired in August 1989 and bought twenty hectares nearby. His son Jeff now runs the farm, so instead of calling cattle, Dave's calling squares again. He starts in on "Form a Star," in the second change.
"Now over the left, all over the hall,
Come back on the right if you can at all,
On to the corners, corners all,
Right hand to your partners, grand chain all,
With a rattle of your toe and a kick of your heel,
And you jigger right around on the back of your heel,
You step right home and swing with your own,
And you leave my dear little honey alone,
All in a ring you promenade all, promenade all.

"The first couple swing on the head,
swing on the head,
Roll to the right and balance there,
Join your hands and circle the half,
Step right and left across to the left,
Across to the left, and balance there,
With your right hands across form a star,
And your left hands back there you are,
Right hand to the lady behind your back,
Left to your own, left to your own,
And swing with your opposite all alone,
Step back home and you swing with your own,
And you leave my dear little honey alone,
Around you go to your places all,
Go right and left across to the head of the hall,
head of the hall,
Right and left back, with a shake of your shoe,
And the two ladies change in the centre change,
Change then back, cut away half,
Go right, go left, go follow the call,
Go over the left in the corners all,
Right hand to your partner, grand chain all,
With your cork leg up and your wooden leg down,
And you hurry right up or you'll never get around,

Dave Duncan

You step right home and you swing with your own,
All in a ring, promenade all, promenade all..."

Dave explains that there are three different types of calls in a square, but he has a hard time explaining it any further; for him it's just a matter of the timing of the music. "Nobody ever explained that part to me. A good caller knows what will go for first, second and the break-down. It goes by the timing. It's not something everyone can do. Some have timing and others don't. If you haven't got any, the dancers will fall over their own feet. The fiddler plays and then I start calling; you don't discuss it ahead of time," says Dave. "You just know."

But Dorothy has studied the calling and squares for years and offers her own explanation of how it works: "We like to have three calls in the square. There's the first, second and third changes. Lots of places just have two changes nowadays. Each of the changes are different types of calls, the first sort of introduces people to each other, like 'Dip for the oyster, Dunk for the clam.' The second is the most difficult. You know, 'Right hand across and form a star, Left hand back and there you are.' And the third is the break-down dance, it's the fastest and you dance with all the partners in your set. It's similar to step-dancing. Might be 'Ladies in the centre, Back to back' or 'Basket Swing.' It looks complicated

The band continually changes during the evening so everyone has a chance to play.

but it's not. They always rhyme and that's part of the fun of it."

Along with the fun comes the complexity of learning to listen, follow directions, and talk - or hoot with laughter - all at the same time.

Dorothy pauses in her conversation to peer out onto the dance-floor at a nearby square whose members are standing helplessly as the caller goes on. Dorothy rushes out to them, grabbing one by the waist, another by the hand, she shows them how it's done. Breathless, she returns to her post by the light switches.

"You watch people square dancing and even a sour one will have a smile on their face. You can't help it," says Dorothy, a spry fifty-two-year-old. "It seems like people were just waiting for a chance to play and sing and dance again."

Bill Stewart, a fifty-nine-year-old Pakenham township councillor says that he keeps his farm down to one hundred and fifteen cows and eight or nine horses. "That's enough for me, I want a bit of energy to square dance. I've never missed one of these monthly dances. Out and around at other dances they won't play a square. They say people won't dance but look at them here. I love the sound of a good fiddler and a good caller."

There's never any shortage of callers. It's not unusual to have five or six on hand. Tonight there's Jim Blair from West Carleton, Dave and Doug Duncan from Pakenham, Dale Bradley of Pakenham, George James from Lanark and Joe Hunt of Arnprior. "We have some great callers around here," says Dave.

Although he won't admit it, Dave ranks with the best. Back in 1949, when he was eighteen years old, Dave earned six dollars a night calling, five

nights a week. He played the Mayfair in Arnprior for the Friday night Midnight Frolicks, and Cobden's Bayview Hall. The owner of the halls, Alex Staye, had three or four bands back then. "I called for Doug Russell. I called for Don Messer two nights, in Arnprior and Cobden. That was when he was a radio personality. His show started at quarter past six and went for fifteen minutes," says Dave.

He's not quite sure how he learned. "I never took lessons. I think we're all the same. You just pick it up from one another." If not his actual teacher, Charlie Finner was certainly Dave's model. "Don Messer said he was one of the best. He was certainly my favourite. He had a roll to his timing. He'd shout for a square on the floor and his voice would ring, it'd ring over the speakers," says Dave.

He also liked the way Charlie used fillers, the little rhymes to help beat off the time in between directions to the dancers: "Up the elm and down the pine, You swing yours and I'll swing mine." "I don't know if I made some up or not. Maybe I heard them somewhere," says Dave.

The repertoire of songs seems endless. "The other night I called six squares, that's eighteen changes and none were the same. There's a lot of different changes, hundreds. I knew one fellow who knew fifty-four different changes. Lots we've forgotten because we haven't used them for years."

Not only are the Pakenham dances a perfect opportunity for the callers, they're also an excellent excuse for musicians to dust off their instruments. "We're not short of nothing to tell you the truth," said Dave. As many as five fiddlers appear on stage. Paul Gemmil, a fiddler from Watsons Corners, got shot in the arm a year ago while deer hunting; his first thought was whether or not he'd be able to fiddle again. He holds his bow at a precarious angle but he's up there now accompanied by fellow fiddlers Lyall Mather from Middleville and George Fife from Union Hall. Larry Lunney plays the piano and Wayne Munro handles the drums. "They're a great group of people who love the music and they're all easy to work with. They don't rehearse nothing. There's enough tunes that everybody knows," says Dave.

The hall's temperature rises noticeably during the first square. A man remarks to his wife: "There's more exhaust fans in a barn than there is in here."

Dave thrives on the crowd. "The hardest thing in the world is to call to one set on the floor, but if you've got eight or ten then it goes, it gets you in the mood to go," he says. "I like to dance but I don't get much chance."

There's no shortage of talent or dancers now, but Dave wonders about the future. Part of his reason for starting the dances was to attract some young people, but grey heads dominate the dance-floor. Dave knows of several remarkable young fiddle players but he only knows of one young caller. "I wish some of the young ones would do it."

All eyes are on John Langford as he does a little step-dancing during the Pakenham Square Dance.

Chapter Five

Beyond the Farm Gate

"I just keep on learning things and making new friends."

Not every young college woman gets a care package from home filled with specimen cob corn, but then not every young woman is as devoted to farming as Jennifer Hyland.

Jennifer, who is nineteen, has been hanging around the barn at Landel Farm since she was a six-month-old baby. She's been competing in agricultural events since she joined the West Rideau Valley 4-H Club in 1983. She took home her first prizes the year after. "I love to farm," she says. "I love the physical labour and working with my hands."

Jennifer is now in her second year at the University of Guelph earning her Bachelor of Science in Agriculture with a major in agricultural economics. She sends home for her produce so she can enter the university's competitions. In her first year she was grand champion in seeds and forages. Although she's not exactly sure what she wants to do when she completes her degree, she knows it will be farming related.

In the family home near Kars, plaques fill a dining-room wall, trophies conceal the organ and hundreds of ribbons dangle from a plant hanger. All belong to Jennifer and her sixteen-year-old brother Jason; most are for agricultural events including 4-H.

Jennifer's résumé reads like a fair-prize list; she seems to have won most everything at some time or another including 4-H awards for top farm-machinery member in Carleton County, top member overall in Rideau Township, most points in 4-H at the Ottawa Valley Farm Show, Nutrite

Award for top 4-H cob corn and top corn overall at the Ottawa Valley Farm Show, and top judging team at the Gloucester Fair.

Jennifer's record in plowing events is impressive too. She placed second in her class at the International Plowing Match in 1984. "The boys didn't like me. Only the guy who beat me would talk to me," she says. Since then, Jennifer has competed in five or ten plowing shows nearly every summer. Usually she places first or second in her class.

Not only is Jennifer involved in the hands-on plowing, she's also actively involved in promoting the events. She's now serving her second term as the Ottawa-Carleton Queen of the Furrow. In this role, she's a guest of honour at agricultural fairs where she hands out ribbons, attends banquets and publicizes plowing.

"I think plowing is a neat sport. I really enjoy it. I like the neatness of a good plowed ridge. It's very precise," says Jennifer.

Jason started participating in plowing events when he was only seven years old. He competed in his first International Plowing Match in 1987. Not surprisingly he was the youngest competitor. Officials were reluctant to let him plow until they saw he could handle the tractor's clutch. Jason won a gold watch that year for his participation as the youngest plower. His mother says, "He'll do anything as long as it has a steering-wheel on it."

Like his sister, Jason has also won a lot of 4-H and fair awards. His crowning achievement came in 1988 when his calf was selected the grand champion for the Scotiabank Hays Classic All-Breed Junior Dairy Show at Ontario's largest fair, the Royal Winter Fair. "It's not difficult to

Jennifer, Jason, Lloyd and Elsie Hyland

train a calf," he says. "The hardest part is getting them to stand in the right place."

Jennifer's and Jason's interest in farming could be partially inherited; they're the fifth generation of Hylands on the farm which dates back one hundred and fifty years. But their interest has also been carefully cultivated and encouraged by their parents, Elsie and Lloyd.

"Both kids are enthusiastic about farming partially because of 4-H and all the opportunities," says Elsie. "Jason loves to get the big ribbons. Both kids are just beaming as they carry ribbons out of the ring. It's so rewarding for them."

Elsie is now a 4-H leader for the West Rideau Valley Club, which has thirteen members in its area between Burritts Rapids, Ottawa and Kemptville. "I like to see the kids enjoying and learning. They get so excited about their Achievement Day. It's very rewarding."

Achievement Day is the high point of the summer for 4-H members. They compete with other 4-H clubs and farmers in their area. Jennifer and Jason go to the Metcalfe Fair. After the local event, winners go on to the Championship Show for Ottawa-Carleton. If they win there, they go on to the Ottawa Winter Fair and the next step is the Royal Winter Fair in Toronto.

The West Rideau Valley Club is one of twenty-five community clubs in Carleton County. About three hundred and fifty members between the ages of ten and twenty-one participate in the various courses. Six-week-long courses are held each fall and spring, and then there are summer-long courses, from April to September, when the 4-H members raise livestock or grow produce to enter at their local agricultural fairs.

Each meeting begins with the 4-H Pledge:
I pledge -
My Head to clearer thinking,
My Heart to greater loyalty,
My Hands to larger service, and
My Health to better living, for
My Club, my Community and my Country.

4-H members complete many projects during the year.

The pledge to head, heart, hands and health make up the four Hs. The club's motto is to learn by doing, but the organization's goal is not just to teach members how to raise the best calf or grow the best corn. The real emphasis is on teaching them to be leading citizens.

Four-H began in Canada in 1913 as Boys' and Girls' Clubs which taught young people about livestock, sewing, foods and gardening. In 1952 the clubs were renamed 4-H and there are now 44,270 members across Canada. In Ontario

15,534 youths belong, and in the Ottawa Valley there are about fifteen hundred members.

The Ontario Ministry of Agriculture and Food trains the volunteer club leaders, provides a local rural leadership co-ordinator and publishes the 4-H manuals. Policies and programs are developed by the Ontario 4-H Council, and individual clubs hold their own fund-raising events.

In the barn, Elsie strides between rows of forty jersey cows, swinging her milking apparatus in front of her and rhyming off the names of the

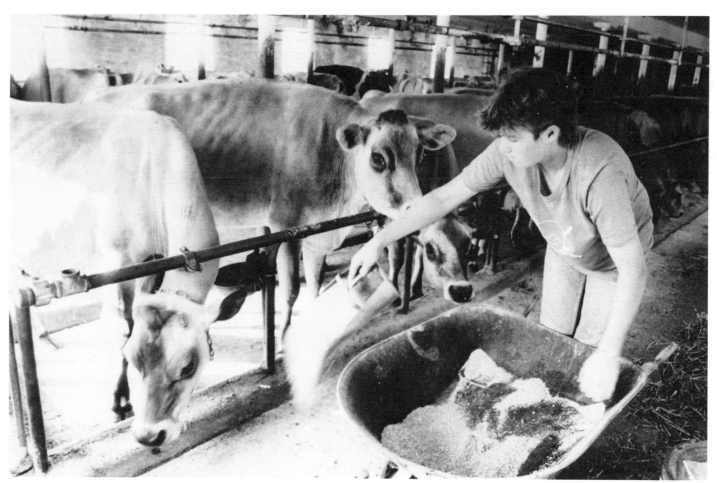

Jason feeds the cows as part of his daily chores.

cows her children have raised for 4-H projects. "There's Spooky, she was born on Hallowe'en day and she never did like to show. That's Trudie and Mamie and Cam, he was eighth at the Royal, and there's Jennifer - that was Jennifer's first 4-H calf."

Inside the Hyland's barn.

Jennifer says that she loves to take care of the cows and watch them grow. She's been the Jersey Princess for eastern Ontario and western Quebec, as well as for the Royal Winter Fair.

"I put Jennifer into 4-H. She was shy and wouldn't speak or anything. Now she's doing really well. Jason was a little shy too but he took part and he's enjoying it. He's been to the Royal twice with calves."

Jennifer says that she's glad her parents convinced her to join. "If it hadn't been for Mom and Dad urging me to try, I'd probably be sitting here at home."

Altogether Jennifer has completed twenty-nine 4-H courses, an average of five or six a year. She hopes to complete her personal goal of forty courses by her twenty-first birthday. Jennifer's 4-H plaque shines with tiny metal tabs listing the names of all her courses: dairy calf, potatoes, seed to shelf, sewing and on and on. This summer she'll add field crop and farm machinery to her list of courses.

"You learn different things each year though there's some overlap. In field crop we're learning about breeding and I'll grow several breeds of cob corn."

She also helps her mother with the local 4-H. As a youth leader, she helps prepare for the meetings, teaches members how to judge livestock and produce, and answers questions. Some day, she says, she plans to be a 4-H leader. "I'd like the chance to put back in what I've taken out of it," she says.

"There are so many opportunities that you can have. I just keep on learning things and making new friends. It's a good start," says Jennifer.

Theodore Beach

"I'd made fifty cents and I thought I had the world by the tail."

Theodore Beach, Oxford Mills

"I started on my own in the fall of '39. I bought the scale house at the stockyards and at that time people would bring livestock there or you'd go out into the country and pick them up. You'd weigh them and pay the people and then you'd ship the livestock to Montreal. We used to load on Monday. At the start, in '39 and '40 and '41, we'd use sleighs in the winter-time and in the spring, wagons. Then as time went on a bit we started to use trucks and we switched from Montreal to Canada Packers in Hull. We went there for years and at the start we used to ship by train. Then by about the '50s they started to phase out the shipping of cattle by train and then we trucked them to Hull. Then on in the '50s they started the sale barns so I was dealing there quite a lot.

"I used to buy everything. Practically every hundred acres there was a farm and back in those days there was somebody on there keeping any place from eight to fifteen cows and the odd one maybe kept twenty or twenty-five. And at that time in this district there was lots of cheese factories and you used to take your milk to the cheese factory from May to November. And you kept a few pigs, always a sow or two, and you raised the pigs and all these little farms they kept a few sheep and a team of horses or three to work the land and that was about the general rule. They seemed to make a living off of it. Nobody had no money, but everybody seemed to live. You had all these little farms that you kept track of and you'd go along. When I started there were three in the business, competing for the livestock from the farmers. You'd pass along each farm and keep track of when their pigs were going to be ready and get in there and try to buy them. There was more competition then, than

there is today. Today there is some country buyers but not all that many. Back in them days some of the farmers would get to like one buyer and they'd tend to stick with that buyer and they'd trust you to give them what it's worth. Then there were other farmers who would have all three in to bid.

"When I think back from when I was ten years old I had it in my mind that I was going to deal in cattle. I can't remember anything else and that's what I did. I never changed my mind. My father was in what you'd call the milk cow business and he dealt in springer cattle before me. I guess that's where I got the training. I can remember the first cow I bought up at the corner here and I gave the man two dollars and a half for it. That was in the '30s and I was twelve years old. I led it from here, I suppose it was three miles, to the stockyards and I always remember Tom saying to me, 'Will your father be in a little later?' And I said, 'Yeah, but this cow belongs to me.' He said, 'How much do you want for it?' And in his next breath he said, 'How much did you pay for it?' And I said, 'Two dollars and a half.' And he said, 'No more.' He just took out three dollars and gave me three dollars and I put it in my pocket and went to school. I'd made fifty cents and I thought I had the world by the tail.

"When I was a kid I remember my father used to assemble twenty to twenty-three cows that he would send to Syracuse. We'd start at five o'clock in the morning and drive them to Prescott, on to the boat and then we'd go over and we'd drive them on up to the stockyards and load them in the cars there. We'd have them loaded by half past two or three o'clock in the afternoon. Dad would have two or three young fellows and actually when I went I wasn't too much good. I went from the time I was six years old. I always loved to go. Mother would pack a great big box full of biscuits and sandwiches, and when we came back — I can see the ice-cream parlour yet just on the corner, just as you come off the boat in Prescott there. Dad always stopped there and we always had a feed of ice cream."

Ken and Kaye Hartin

"...no one realizes the opportunities a country veterinarian has to help."

Ken Hartin, Richmond

"One night in the fall of the year when they were threshing we were putting the cows in to milk them and it was late and who comes in but some cattle dealers. They were picking out some of the best cows and they were paying a hundred and eighty dollars for a cow. Dollars were hard to come by and I knew my father didn't want to sell his best cow but he ended up doing it for twenty dollars more. I didn't realize how scarce dollars were but I said to myself, if I could ever get in the position where I could help people to make decisions which would make their life easier, I would do it. I wasn't thinking about being a veterinarian that night but no one realizes the opportunities a country veterinarian has to help. There was lots of challenges and lots of opportunities.

"We did mostly farm work. There was a lot of emergencies like with cows with prolapsed uterus or calving cases and they would like you to be there right now. A lot of them would call as soon as they got up, but you answered the phone no matter when it rang, at night or in the daytime, and you tried to satisfy these emergencies. It's a way of life. If you liked it, it was very saitisfying. I'd go out and do calls but the phone would still ring and people would come in to get medicine.

"People would pay you a compliment or when you'd come out there'd be a couple of frozen steaks on the seat of the truck. Someone phoned me up over at the airport one night and he had an animal he was excited about and we went over and did a Caesarean on it at two o'clock in the morning. Afterwards, I said to him, 'I hope you've got some gasoline. I don't have enough to get home.' And he said, 'I don't either but you take my car and bring it back in the morning.' And so I came back in the morning and there was a forty-ounce bottle of B and G Scotch sitting on the truck seat. If I'd had that much gasoline I could've driven home.

"In those times we didn't know that cows ate nails and that because they were looking for phosphorus. There were mineral deficiencies and the farmers got to realize if you left your sweaty shirt or your gloves down, your cows would eat them because they were looking for salt. But once they learned to practise preventive medicine they would give them minerals and the cattle didn't have that depraved appetite.

"In those days we were on a party line. There must have been fifteen people on the line and some young person would be talking on the phone and central would ring in and ring our number and the young people would stop talking and we would get the message to go somewhere because they had a cow calving and the young people would keep on talking as soon as we hung up again. Sometimes Kay would be out and no one would be here to answer the phone and so the operator, Miss Mulligan, would say Mr. Hartin is out at either this farm or that farm. Then she would phone that farm. We think things are modern and efficient today but we have no idea how efficient they used to be."

Allan Byrnes admiring the old machinery at the Merrickville Fair held in August 1990.

Finley McEwen positions his antique farm machine.

Equipment displays are always popular at the fair.

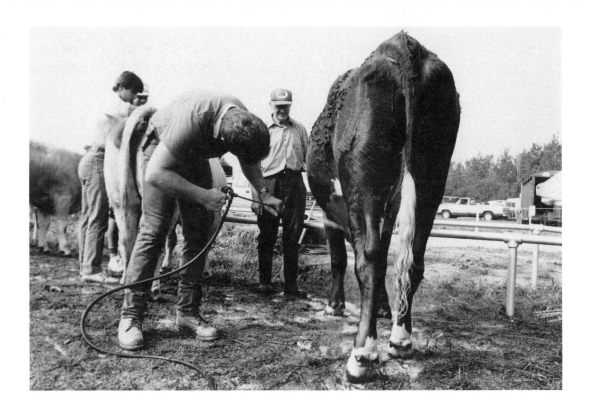

Cattle are washed and groomed before each showing.

There is a lot of activity before competition begins.

Careful attention is given to every detail.

A moment to relax before entering the show ring.

4-H club members preparing to go into the ring.

A young 4-H competitor at the Merrickville Fair.

256

Everyone hopes to impress the judges.

The contestants are of all ages.

Everyone is a judge at the Merrickville Fair.

The judge makes his final decision.

Finley McEwen proudly displays his machinery at the Merrickville Fair.

Arnold Mitchell exhibits his 1926 Waterloo.

Cyril Greene

"I always loved horses..."

Cyril Greene, Kinburn

"I was born on this farm, right upstairs. We kept cattle and horses and pigs. I remember when we'd take a wagon load of pork and chickens in the fall and sell it on the market. We used to have an old threshing mill and an old tractor. I'd be twelve or thirteen or so and we used to go and do threshing for people to get a few dollars. We had a few good Holstein cows, maybe twelve or maybe more sometimes, and at night mother would have to milk by herself; there was no milking-machines. We'd come home at eight o'clock at night or so and she'd have all those cows milked.

"I bought my first team in 1968. I always loved horses and I like the Clydes; they're a good sensible horse and I like the white legs. Everybody likes their own. Some people they like Belgians; another guy likes percherons.

"I sell cattle and feed cattle too. Another guy and I have a feedlot in Peterborough. We feed as high as five hundred head. I bought for Crabtree Meat Packers for twenty some years. I used to go to all the sales. This country is full of cattle but the poor farmers aren't making any money; they're getting out. Western Canada and western United States and every country you want to mention is pluggin' beef in here and so they don't need any cattle. And it costs so much to operate around here with the cold weather and our fuel is crazy and tires and parts and new machinery — you can't do it; that's all there is to it; you just can't do it. We've got a great bunch of farmers around here — good, hard-working lads that will work day and night — but there's no money in it."

Cyril out in the field with some of his Clydesdale horses.

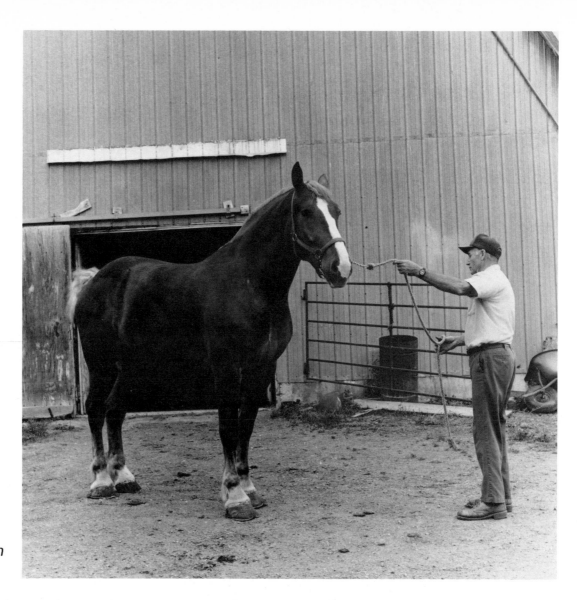

Stewart shows one of his twenty-four Belgian horses.

"I was the blacksmith."

Stewart Crabb, Stittsville

"I have twenty-four horses at the present time, all Belgians. The first horse I got was back in about '54. I got one from Wyman Davidson out there; it was a half-breed colt. I worked with the Mounted Police there from the fall of '59 and I quit in 1981. I was the blacksmith. I don't do much anymore, just my own. I just took a notion that I wanted to learn the trade and at that time they were looking for men at the Mounted Police and so I got there and worked under John Dunlop. I've farmed here since 1970. I was raised down on the other farm, straight behind us here. I used to do a bit of custom work but you get fed up. It would be eleven or twelve o'clock when I came home. You'd come home and do your bit of chores and then someone would call you and you'd go shoe some horses. Horses were always on the farm and it gets into your blood. Those trophies have been building up probably since '64."

Stewart Crabb

An auction sale has become a common sight along many farm roads.

A story behind every article for sale.

The final items on the block.

The crowd gathers to look over some of the goods.

The auctioneer tries to get the best price.

A closer look before bidding.

There is always an auction to be found.

Auctions draw people from all walks of life.

Peter and Morris Barr

"We can't compete here with the subsidies..."

Morris Barr, Galetta

"We've had the sale barns here since 1973, and since 1975 in Cobden. We were farming across the river and we moved there in 1960. We started milking cows and we milked there till '71 then we sold the milkers off and we were in beef till '73. 'Seventy-seven was the biggest year in cattle in the way of volume we had go through here. From '77 till today it's been on a decline because so many farmers have retired. When we came here there was about five plants in Ottawa and they all bought cattle here and now there's really none of them left in the area. The biggest change was when we lost all those packing plants. The beef that's sold out of here goes to Montreal and some of it goes to Toronto. Our son lives right beside us here and he's been with us in the business since we came here. The other son lives at Cobden and he looks after up there and we just go up on sale day.

"The farmers come here to check the markets and a lot come to visit their neighbours. It used to be that the calves from the west came out here to Ontario to be fed and slaughtered. Now the western governments are paying subsidies on the grain and they're paying subsidies on the beef and so they're building bigger slaughter plants out there and easterners are buying boxed meat. We can't compete here with the subsidies they're paying out there because Ontario's not paying subsidies on the grain and they're not paying subsidies on the beef."

The front row is reserved for livestock dealers at the Galetta Sales Barn.

A twenty-five-hundred-pound bull attracts the attention of several dealers.

Morris Barr owns the Galetta Sales Barn in West Carleton.

Gerald Walsh

"It's really a social event."

Gerald Walsh, Osceola

"I'm a livestock dealer and auctioneer. We do two horse sales a year. I buy and sell cattle on a daily basis and then we do auctions here. The horse sales always attract large crowds. The husband and wife come, three or four kids and grandpa and grandmother, the whole works. We give out maybe two hundred and twenty buyer numbers but for every buyer number there's probably six people. It's just a big day out and the most expense they have is the sandwich or the hot dog. It's really a social event. The old-fashioned farm sale you start in the granary with the tools and then you do the household stuff and then you go to the farm machinery - and you always kick off the farm machinery with the tractor - and then to the cattle.

"I owned calves here when I was twelve years old. Then I started dealing in cattle. I'd take the car and take a Saturday afternoon and go and buy two baby pigs for four dollars each and put them in the wood-shed or someplace until Tuesday and then take them to the sale barns to see if I could make a little bit. When I was in high school I'd skip the last two classes on Tuesday afternoon and go to the sale barn. Then I got out of school and worked for eighteen months. I didn't make big wages but I made enough to buy a '69 one-ton truck. When the eighteen months were up and I had the money for the truck I left and hit the back country buying cattle."

271

Lorne Wade

"...half a dozen bridles hanging on the wall."

Lorne Wade, Russell

"I originally started in the hardware business. The former shoe repairman and harness maker from town was in this shop cattycorner from my hardware store. I had known this man all my life. He came in one night and said, 'Lorne, why don't you get some shoe-repair equipment in the basement. This community could use that kind of service,' he said. 'I will show you anything about it I know.' Strange as it may seem, the thought had been in the back of my mind, but that was as far as it went. Anyway, unfortunately that man, very shortly after, got killed in a car accident just down the road here. But anyway, it didn't dampen my ambition, and I went ahead and bought the equipment, and his wife was kind enough, she gave me some of the tools that he had. I got to the point where I was really enjoying it. I was up home at the farm and I got the old set of harness; my dad and I brought it in and took it all apart, patched it up and repaired it, and that's really how I got started in harness. There was a time when I had a half a dozen bridles hanging on the wall: tugs, back pads, lines, belly-bands, martingales — I had everything you'd need for a set of harness and, one at a time, I sold them, and I quit making them, and the demand has dropped off."

Lorne still makes the occasional harness.

Bert and Allan Lowry's Penlow Farms on Highway 15 near Carleton Place was the site of the 1990 Lanark County Plowing Match.

Single-furrow plowing is always a popular event.

A plowman is proud of his team.

Single-furrow plowing takes patience and skill.

Sizing up the competition.

The Lanark County Plowing Match attracts many competitors.

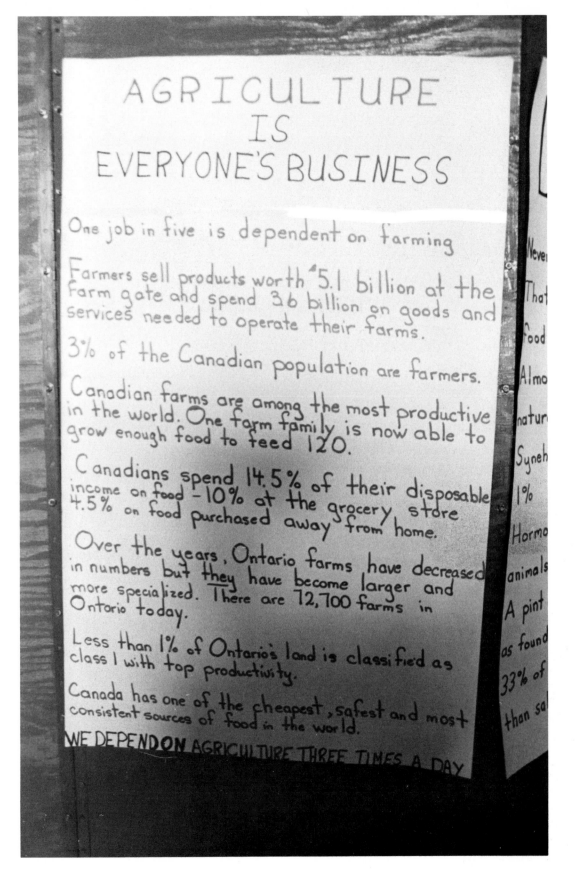

Agriculture Is
Everyone's Business.

Looking over the antique equipment.

On the side of an antique thresher.

Plowmen examine a fresh furrow.

Len McCoy enjoys talking about his Eagle 1925 tractor.

Dad offers words of advice.

A competitor concentrates on his work.

Trina Code was Queen of the Furrow at the Lanark County Plowmen Assocation's Plowing Match.

*Most walking plows
are now used for
competition only.*

An experienced observer.

Ab Sack

"Then, we took a pride in it."

Ab Sack, Pembroke

"I've been in the cattle business now since I was sixteen and I'm fifty-four now. I've worked in beef but I was in the buying end and slaughtering end. I used to work with my dad and then I went on my own and that's how I got into cutting. Livestock was my main end and I've seen a lot of guys come and go.

"We have cows of our own too but I job them all out, winter them all out on these farms and then again in the summer. I don't own the farms, I just rent them. That way I get away from buying expensive machinery and all this, and I let other people do the work. You're only using a lot of them machines a week or two in the year and the rest of the time they're sitting there doing nothing and so I'm better to hire someone to do it and I don't have to build sheds for them or nothing.

"The actual slaughtering of beef hasn't changed. Now they have knock boxes and all power winches, we never had any of that. We split them by hand, we winched them up by hand, and everything was done by hand. Years ago we used to slaughter at night, before inspection came in, and we'd do our day's work and kill anywhere from twenty to thirty-seven head of cattle in a

Ab gets ready to pick up some livestock.

night and be back to work the next morning at seven o'clock. I've worked when we used to slaughter it, hang it in the basement overnight, and then cut it the next morning and take it down to the market. We had no refrigeration, no nothing. Then we got ice and that was a big thing. Then we used to kill a day or two ahead. We used to custom-cut ice along with what we needed for our own use. At that time the blocks were twenty-four by twenty-four, for a cent a block. That's what we used to get for it. For every hundred blocks you'd get one dollar. We'd cut all day long from daybreak in the morning till dark at night. I remember we used to go to the market and all this meat was cut and put on a nice white cloth and everything was handled with care and looked good. Then, we took a pride in it. We've done that here. We keep the place clean and take care of the meat because we grew up in that.

"I would say, and this might sound crazy to some people, but a Holstein cow bred to a Hereford bull and you raise that calf and that's your best meat. It's white and the grain isn't heavy on it."

"No one's going to sell us except ourselves."

Miles of farmland and Ottawa skyscrapers physically separate Meredith Brophy and Theresa Ruiter, but in spirit and philosophy the women are neighbours. Both are concerned with educating people about farming and, in the process, improving the farmers' image. It's more than just a coincidence that both women also have a background in the Junior Farmers' Association of Ontario. They have taken to heart the Junior Farmers' motto: Self-help and Community Betterment.

"Too often farmers are depicted as 'hicks' with straw hats and overalls. They are not. They're business people," says Theresa Ruiter, an active Junior Farmers' member, mother of three young children and partner with her husband Bert on their two-hundred-and-ten-acre dairy farm near Ramsayville.

Meredith Brophy, a retired Junior Farmer, echoes Theresa's concerns. "The stereotypical farmer is nothing like what the farmer has to be today," says Meredith, who works three days a week as a legal secretary, looks after her five-year-old son Conor, and helps her husband Michael operate their eighty-five-acre beef and poultry farm near Osgoode.

"We have to overcome the negative image we have. Farming isn't all smelly clothes and dirty hands," says Meredith. "There are many people in my father-in-law's generation who didn't go past grade eight because they were needed at home, but most people my age who are farming are university graduates. We need education.

Farmers have to be mechanics, electricians, plumbers, business managers, accountants, animal-husbandry experts, crop specialists and carpenters. You have to be a very creative person."

Theresa and Meredith both see children as the key to changing the way people view farmers and the industry. "I don't know how to educate adults about farming," says Meredith. "With children you can work through the education system. It's not going to change overnight but we're trying."

Theresa is the co-founder and acting chairperson of the Ottawa-Carleton Agriculture Awareness Committee and she is also putting together a teachers' resource manual and speakers list.

"There's a real need for this. At the Ottawa Winter Fair we would hear children saying that the cow with the largest horn would win, that chickens lay five eggs a day," says Theresa. "Agriculture is the second-largest industry, next to the civil service, in Ottawa-Carleton. If you eat, then you are a part of the food chain and are therefore involved with agriculture. No one's going to sell us except ourselves," she says.

Theresa's leadership skills and much of her expertise come from her thirteen-year involvement with Junior Farmers' Association of Ontario. She's been the Zone One (eastern Ontario) chairman, zone secretary, South Carleton Club president and county newsletter editor. Today, Theresa is the zone publicity chairman, and March Confrerence administrator. She is one of six hundred Junior Farmers in Zone One, who make up twenty per cent of the total provincial membership which is divided into seven geographical zones.

Michael, Conor and Meredith Brophy

Meredith was also extremely active during her fourteen years as a Junior Farmer, and was inducted into the zone's Junior Farmers' Hall of Fame in 1989. She joined in 1970 so she could curl another night each week and, by the time she retired in 1984, she had been president of the East Carleton Club, Zone One provincial director, and Ontario vice-president, president and past-president. "Each position seemed to be a logical step. I was interested in improving my leadership skills and that was the way to do it," says Meredith.

Now, at age thirty-five, she is a 4-H life-skills leader for the twenty-member Dalmeny club, chairperson of the Metcalfe Fair Board's educational exhibits committee, and chairperson of promotions and advertising for the Ottawa Winter Fair. "It's only natural that agricultural societies should link in with what's being taught in school. My job at the Metcalfe Fair Board is to make sure schools are aware of our programs and to get the children out to our fair to see the exhibits."

"My biggest concern now is in educating the public," says Meredith. "We need education on what farming is today. You don't just go out with a pail and milk a cow, you have forty or fifty cows and that's a lot different."

Through their involvement in the Junior Farmers' Assocaition both Meredith and Theresa have learned more about farming here and in other countries. They believe there will always be a need for the Junior Farmers' Association.

Junior Farmers began in York County in 1914 with a group of young agriculture students who saw a need to educate others about new developments in areas such as erosion and swine-herd viral outbreaks. It remained a county-based organization until 1944 when the provincial body was established in Guelph.

Today there are three thousand Junior Farmers across the province though a decade ago there were eight thousand. The rapid decline in membership reflects the decline in farm population.

Junior Farmers, who are between the ages of fifteen and twenty-nine, concentrate on developing the skills which will make rural and urban people into leaders. They are, by definition, active in their association; when Meredith was provincial president, she was out five nights a week on Junior Farmers' business. Members choose their area of involvement, whether it's organizing a sports event, hosting a dance for a farmer whose barn has burned down, working the gates at a local fair, helping others learn about agricultural judging, raising money for a charity or taking part in an international exchange.

"My mother says my personality changed when I went to the Junior Farmers' leadership camp in 1971," says Meredith. "I was shy before that; I wasn't interested in joining anything. It does wonders for your self-confidence, that's the main thing."

As Theresa faces her final two years in Junior Farmers, she plans to continue to take advantage of as many programs as possible. She's anxious to get accepted into the acclaimed Advanced Agriculture Leadership Program, a two-year education and travel program aimed at developing leaders who will shape the future. "I hope it will give me some direction on how I can make a difference," says Theresa.

Bert, Theresa, Megan, Cayse and Bryson Ruiter

Junior Farmers make a big difference in their own communities where members help out and raise money for charity. In 1989 the provincial association raised more than thirty thousand dollars for the Canadian Guide Dogs for the Blind. Valley fund-raising events have included car rallies, strawberry socials, dances, petting zoos and cow-chip bingo. Junior Farmers also offer their help at various charitable events such as telethons and Ottawa's Terry Fox Run, and they sponsor their own events such as Hallowe'en and Christmas parties for children.

Both women say that they appreciate the leadership skills they have acquired, but equally important to them are the friends they have made through social and sporting events. "Junior Farmer friends are forever," says Meredith. "When an ex-member gets married now, it's like a Junior Farmers' reunion."

Theresa's husband, thirty-one-year-old Bert, jokingly refers to the Junior Farmers as the "marriage club." "You meet so many people that you can't help but find someone special," he says.

"You tend to meet people with common interests at Junior Farmers' functions," says Meredith, who met her husband Michael at an association function. "You get to make friends with people from all over."

Functions vary according to the interests of members at the club, county and zone levels. Some functions prepare members to take part in the five Junior Farmers' provincial events including the organizational March Conference.

The Summer and Winter Games include traditional sports such as curling, softball, hockey and broomball, as well as farm-related events such as the Farm Safety Competitions, a tractor rodeo and the Farmers' Olympics. Members also compete in quizzes and public speaking to obtain the coveted Super Farmer of the Year award.

At Sing Swing, members yodel, sing, whistle and dance for fun and awards. And at Culturama, public speaking, spelling-bees, poetry writing and recitation, doodlemania, one-act plays, slide presentations and the farmers' feud quiz competition are just some of the events.

"They encourage you to participate. To speak, act, sing or whatever in public," says Theresa. Last year she came in second in public speaking and took home first for her slide presentation on her Junior Farmers' social and cultural exchange to the Republic of Ireland in July 1989. "The exchanges let us see how people around the world deal with things on the farm and in the community," Theresa says.

Meredith took part in exchanges with similar rural youth groups in Indiana, Missouri and Washington, D.C. "The contact with different organizations allowed me to find out how they work. Future Farmers of America in Washington, D.C., was very organized. There was lots to learn," said Meredith.

"I'm sure I got more out of Junior Farmers than I was able to put in," says Meredith.

Index

(Photo Credit) T. Kelly

About The Author

Steve Evans is renowned for his documentary photographs and oral histories of the Ottawa Valley people. The Back Forty: Farm Life in the Ottawa Valley is his third pictorial collection. His first two books, Heart and Soul: Portraits of Canada's Ottawa Valley and Up the Line: More Portraits of the Ottawa Valley, were both Canadian bestsellers.

An Ottawa Valley native, Steve was born in Richmond, Ontario in 1955. His interest in photography began in 1975. Steve and his wife Teresa live in Richmond.

For the more than 3,000 photographs taken for this book, Steve used a Hasselblad two-and-a-quarter camera and a Nikon 35mm camera with Ilford film and paper.